Library of
Davidson College

DATA CONVERSION

by
Ruth C. Carter
and
Scott Bruntjen

Appendixes compiled by Elaine Rast

Knowledge Industry Publications, Inc.
White Plains, NY and London

Professional Librarian Series

Data Conversion

Library of Congress Cataloging in Publication Data

Carter, Ruth C.
　　Data conversion.

　　(Professional librarian series)
　　Bibliography: p.
　　Includes index.
　　1. Machine-readable bibliographic data.　　I. Bruntjen,
Scott.　II. Title.　III. Series.
Z699.C38　1983　　025.3'028'54　　83-84
ISBN 0-86729-047-1
ISBN 0-86729-046-3 (pbk.)

Printed in the United States of America

Copyright © 1983 by Knowledge Industry Publications, Inc., 701 Westchester Ave., White Plains, NY 10604. Not to be reproduced in any form whatever without written permission from the publisher.

10　9　8　7　6　5　4　3　2　1

Table of Contents

Introduction 1
1. The Purpose of Data Conversion 3
2. Planning for Data Conversion: Project Analysis 21
3. Planning for Data Conversion: Project Design 45
4. Special Considerations 61
5. Comparison of Data Conversion Methods 77
6. Pitfalls 89
7. Summary and Outlook 99
Appendix A: Libraries That Have Implemented Data Conversion Projects 105
Appendix B: Consultants on Data Conversion 145
Appendix C: Vendors of Data Conversion Services 151
Bibliography 161
Index 167
About the Authors 169

List of Figures

Figure 1.1: Elements of an Integrated System 5
Figure 1.2: Schematic Representation of the Bibliographic Information Interchange Format from the ANSI Standard Z39.2 7
Figure 1.3: The MARC Record as It Appears in OCLC 8
Figure 1.4: The MARC Record as It Would Appear on the Tape 9
Figure 1.5: A Typical Bar Code 14
Figure 5.1: Data Conversion Cost Analysis Worksheet 82

Introduction

Data conversion for libraries is the process of turning non-computer-readable library records into a computer-readable format. The process can apply to all elements used in library files and records, but this book will be concerned primarily with bibliographic information.

This book presents the philosophical and theoretical issues, while emphasizing the practical requirements for data conversion in libraries. It will help the reader to organize and conduct an effective conversion effort as well as to understand the larger issues of data control, access and dissemination. This work is introductory in nature. For the reader not experienced in data conversion it should serve as a basic source. For the more experienced reader it should serve as a refresher of basic concepts. More advanced texts and sources are mentioned in the notes and bibliography. The following major points are included within this work:

1. Advantages of data conversion, with a description of the new or enhanced capabilities available after conversion;

2. Steps in planning conversion;

3. Consideration of external factors, such as standards;

4. Description and comparison of resources required in various approaches to conversion, including the production of detailed cost proposals;

5. Implementing the conversion process;

6. Working with library materials that require special considerations;

7. Becoming familiar with the basic elements of the MARC record;

8. Using the major bibliographic utilities to support conversion projects;

9. Relating new technology to traditional library information;

10. Pitfalls of data conversion.

One might question this preoccupation with the change of format of traditional library information. The change represents no new ideas, but only a new and more powerful way of expressing how libraries have attempted to describe to their patrons the resources that they hold. Now, however, libraries have the chance to know something more about their resources, about their patrons and about how their collections and patrons interact. Libraries now have the chance to exploit their collections in ways that were not possible before. Libraries now have an opportunity to build regional collections even though they remain independent institutions. Through the data conversion process, librarians have the opportunity to interact with the new technology and, unfortunately, to make immediately visible and expensive mistakes.

Since conversion offers the extremes of potential success and disaster, the topic deserves a practical text. What follows is a discussion of the practical in the context of the philosophical. Both are essential if librarians are to use this new capability to the best advantage.

1
The Purpose of Data Conversion

Before starting a data conversion effort, it is essential to have a sense of what all of the final products should be and should look like. Throughout the history of cataloging rules, libraries have cataloged and recataloged and re-recataloged. For example, in the late 1960s many academic and public libraries changed from the Dewey Decimal System to the Library of Congress Classification System. It is a major mission of this book to help prevent the 1990s from being filled with reconversion. Once is enough, as you may already know or will come to find out.

There has already been some reconversion activity. Libraries whose early circulation systems built their data bases from the data found on charge-out cards discovered later that staff and patrons liked using the entire data base as a sort of online catalog. Unfortunately, essential elements were missing (publisher, date, much of the title, established main entries, to name a few) and this made the online "catalog" not very useful. Many libraries made the mistake of automating a manual routine without considering what would be possible, what would be nice to have and what might be rethought. They now must consider a reconversion of the data to a standard form.

Interestingly enough, a total systems approach is not new. Librarians have thought of the total range of end applications almost every time they created a new way of controlling information. Planning in the manual environment is common. What happened in the implementation of early automation was the abandonment of certain basic library principles. It is time to review them.

THE CENTRAL ROLE OF THE CATALOG

With the advent of the card catalog and with the adoption of standard cataloging rules, libraries became able to support a totally integrated system. The library's catalog formed the data base of that system. The rules for entering data into that system were highly refined. There were rules for classification, for establishing the entry, for describing the item and for adding other entry points in the data base. There were entry authorities and there were subject authorities. There were rules for formatting the data on the card, and for filing the cards and thus building the data base.

The catalog became the focus for access to a collection, but it also began to serve as the data base from which other products were developed. The charge-out card data were developed as by-products of the cataloging information. The entry and the title might be briefer than those found in the catalog but both subsets were derived from the catalog data. To help locate materials in special places, flags were often added to the catalog. A plastic jacket signaled the fact that a library had placed this item temporarily in a special collection ("Reserve") or announced that the material was in a medium other than print. The acquisitions department often got into the act by placing on-order information in the catalog, so that staff and patrons alike could know that something was expected to arrive later.

Some libraries added special cards with serial entries, so that readers could ascertain which issues of a serial had arrived. In at least one library, such cards were placed at each and every entry point in the catalog, so that specific information about every issue was present. This certainly represented a lot of labor but it also provided a lot of convenient information; more important, library staff realized that the catalog was the accessible data base which contained all there was to know about the collection.

The data elements on the book card that were used to describe the item charged out were extracted from and were verified by the catalog entry. The author and title as provided on the book card and the book pocket agreed with the catalog entry although the information was often abbreviated. In sum, the catalog provided the most information about the library's collection, and served as the final authority on the correct way to present this information.

The task of data conversion is to ensure that the authority, comprehensiveness and interrelatedness of the catalog are maintained while increased searching and data interchange capabilities are added. This may not seem difficult, but it has been forgotten more times than not in library conversion plans.

Throughout the process of bibliographic data conversion the catalog information must remain central. Short cuts and practices that may reduce cost and time initially will only add problems later. The conversion process replaces and expands the information that took years of effort to develop. It has the potential to be highly beneficial and it has the potential to be a disaster.

THE TOTAL INTEGRATED SYSTEM

One cannot stress too often the interrelatedness of library information. Conversion projects may be expensive, but their cost must be compared with that of the development of the original data to be converted. Careful planning, thought and work are important in manipulating and replacing that expensive product, the catalog.

Figure 1.1 shows the elements of an integrated system. Essentially, the catalog should be the central focus of data development and interchange both inside the library and

Figure 1.1 Elements of an Integrated System

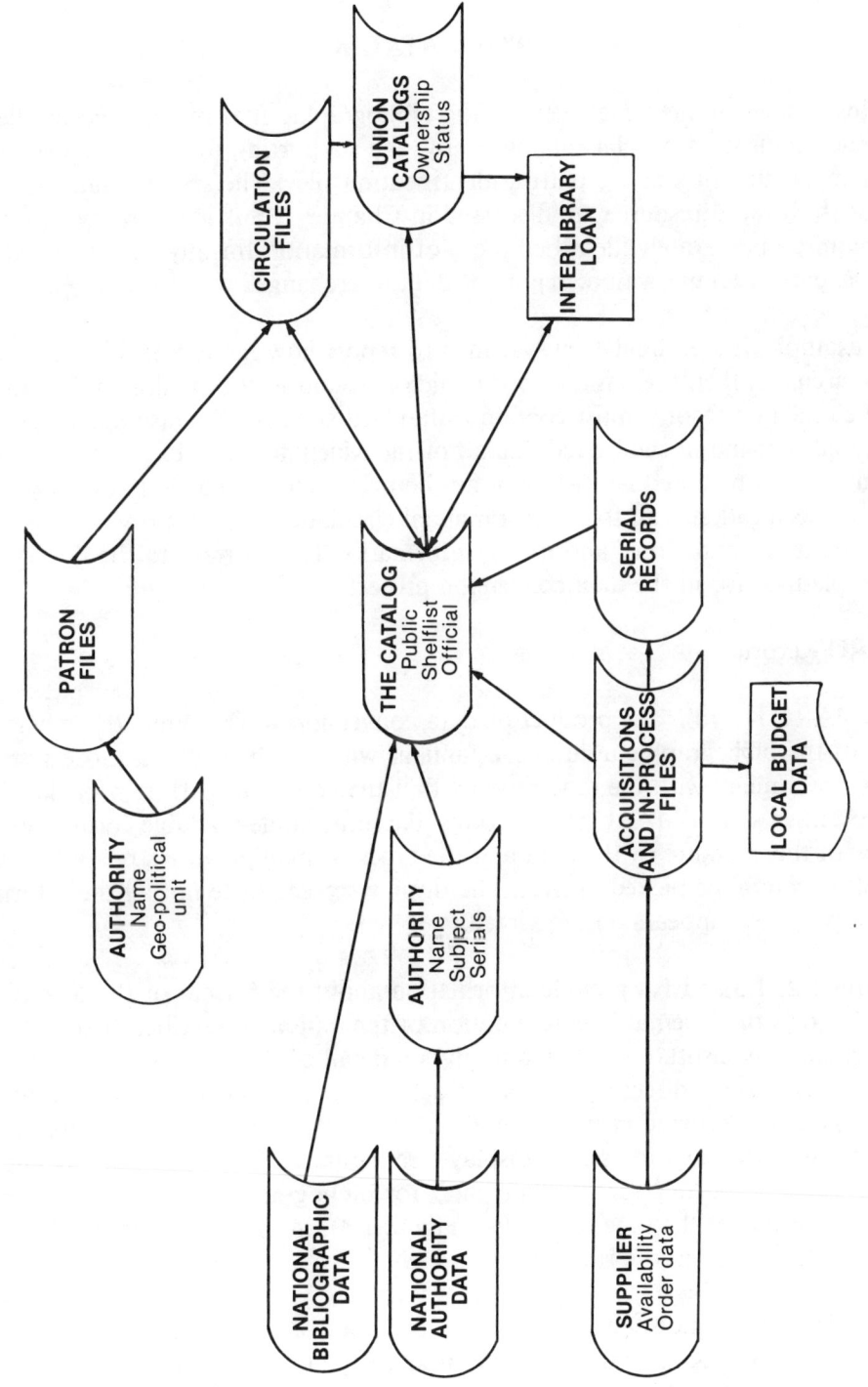

among various libraries. The remainder of this chapter will concentrate on those elements and their relationships, and will stress how data conversion in one place can have an effect elsewhere within the system.

THE CATALOG

In this instance the *catalog* refers to the bibliographic files represented by the public catalog, the shelflist, an official catalog if any, the supporting files for authority control and such supporting files as the patron identification files. The specific data elements required for this central resource are discussed in Chapter 3. Suffice it to say here that the catalog requires a separately identified piece of information for any function that might be required as part of an extraction, report or data interchange.

For example, if the circulation system is to report how many Spanish-language materials circulate, then the basic record (which is found in the catalog and extracted to form the circulation record) must contain a standard code for Spanish-language materials. This material is found in the "fixed fields" of the Machine-Readable Cataloging (MARC) record but, as will be noted later, it may not be present in the converted record unless the conversion specifications call for it. If a manual circulation system provides the number of Spanish-language circulations, and if that information is important to the library, then it should be planned for in the data conversion project.

The MARC Record

The MARC record is the product of data conversion work. While those who have used any of the bibliographic utilities are familiar with the display that those systems produce, few are familiar with the tape product that the conversion effort provides. It is important to know what a MARC record looks like in machine-readable form, and to be familiar with the structure of the data and the types of manipulations possible. This information often cannot be picked up from the display screen, since not all the information on the final tape record appears on the screen.

Figures 1.2, 1.3 and 1.4 provide information about the format of the MARC record. Figure 1.2 shows the schematic representation of the data as prescribed by the American National Standards Institute (ANSI), and gives a detail of the first two areas of information: the leader and the directory. From the detail of the leader, one can see that character positions 5, 6 and 7 provide information about status, type of record and bibliographic level. From the corresponding screen display (see Figure 1.3) one can pick out the codes "n" for record status, "a" for type and "m" for bibliographic level. These codes can be seen in the first line of the tape record (see Figure 1.4), in the 5th, 6th and 7th positions, as one would expect from the standard.

However, some data essential to the conversion effort do not display on the screen. For example, in looking at character position 22 of the tape, one finds "X'Ø1'" which, in this case, is defined by OCLC to mean "produce catalog cards for main holding library or first holding library in 049 field and set user holdings symbol in Online Union Catalog." In subsequent uses of this same record, this transaction code could mean update or cancel.

Figure 1.2 Schematic Representation of the Bibliographic Information Interchange Format from the ANSI Standard Z39.2

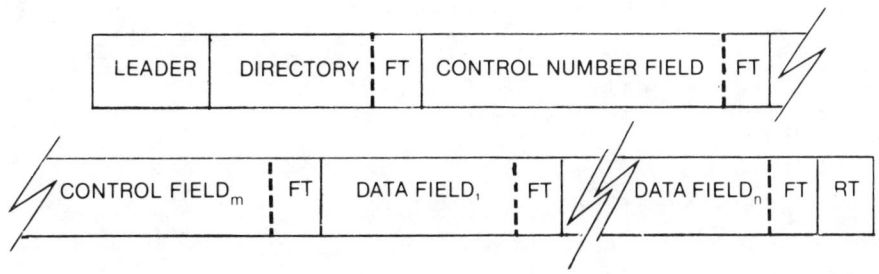

Detail of the "Leader"

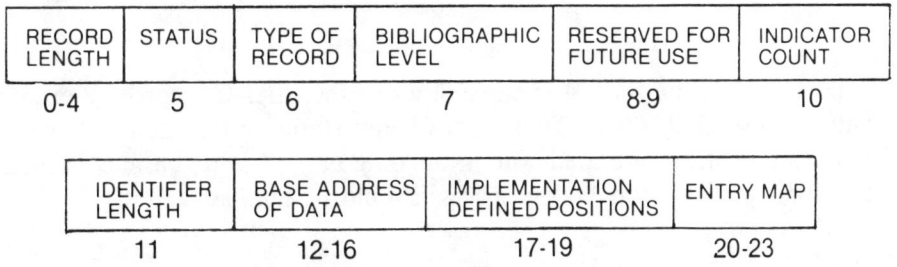

Detail of the "Directory" Giving Structure of Each Entry

TAG	LENGTH OF FIELD (NOTE 1)	STARTING CHARACTER POSITION (NOTE 1)	IMPLEMENTATION DEFINED PORTION (NOTE 2)

While this instruction would not display on the screen, it would be essential for the processing of the tape record if one were attempting to load a local system.

By using the screen display with the tape record in conjunction with the ANSI schematic, one can begin to have an appreciation for the product produced by the conversion effort—the MARC record. The reference shelf of any conversion project should include the current edition of the ANSI Standard Z39.2 "American National Standard for Bibliographic Information Interchange on Magnetic Tape," in addition to the tape subscription service documentation available from the bibliographic utility or vendor supplying the machine-readable tape.

Figure 1.3 The MARC Record as It Appears in OCLC

```
NO HOLDINGS IN OCL -  FOR HOLDINGS ENTER dh DEPRESS   DISPLAY RECD SEND
  OCLC: 491759        Rec stat: n Entrd: 721110         Used: 821109
Type: a Bib lvl: m Govt pub: + Lang:  eng Source: u Illus:
Repr:   Enc lvl: I Conf pub: + Ctry:   +++ Dat tp: + M/F/B: +++
Indx: + Mod rec: + Festschr: + Cont:
Desc:   Int lvl:   Dates: 1970,++++
  1 010
  2 040      +c CCL
  3 090      PS3561.08+b P3 1970
  4 090      +b
  5 049      OCLC
  6 100 10   Kosinski, Jerzy N,+d 1933-
  7 245 1    The painted bird,+c by Jerzy Kosinski.
  8 260 0    New York,+b The Modern Library+c [1970]
  9 300      234 p.+c 22 cm.
```

It is important that the form and capabilities of the MARC record are examined concurrently with the use of this text. That record is not static, in that new data elements are validated and modifications are made on an ongoing basis, but its basic concept is permanent and any manager of a conversion process should be familiar with it.

Authority Files

Libraries have been concerned for years about the importance of authority control of elements that have to file together. When catalogs were in manual form it was important to have all materials about a subject or all materials by a particular author together. The concept of authority files developed so that a group of catalogers, or one cataloger over time, could be consistent in the use of such elements as series title entries, subject headings, form of the author's name used, etc. Certain data conversion systems allow easy changes in the information once it is entered, but the basic premise remains. If one wants all the information to come out together, one must first define how it is entered. If it is all entered in the same way, then retrieval is that much easier. Authority files may be easier to establish and maintain in a manual environment but the requirement for them is not abandoned when one converts.

Total data conversion can include consideration of the need for authority file conversion. If authority files are converted, then they can be easily updated and checked, but their conversion then becomes another part of the total data conversion effort. The data for such authorities as used by the Library of Congress are available for purchase and are loaded for use on the major bibliographic utilities. The forms for these data, like the form for the bibliographic data, are well defined and controlled and should be examined before any local data conversion effort is begun.

Figure 1.4 The MARC Record as It Would Appear on the Tape

```
ØØ41Ønambb22ØØ145IØb45X'01'ØØØ1Ø

Ø13ØØØØØØØ8ØØ41ØØØ13Ø4ØØØ13ØØØ

54Ø9ØØØ23ØØØ67Ø92ØØ23ØØØ9Ø1ØØØ

Ø3ØØØ11324 5ØØ42ØØ14326ØØØ5ØØØ1

853ØØØØ19ØØ23559ØØØ11ØØ254X'1E'0

CL7Ø491759b72111Øc197Ø1965n

yubbbbbbbbbØØØ11bengbuX'1F'bb

X'1F'cCCLX'1F'dGOGX'1E'bbX'1F'aPS3561.

08X'1F'bP3b197ØX'1E'bbX'1F'a813.54X'1F'

bK68p,b1965X'1E'1ØX'1F'aKosinski,b

JerzybN,X'1F'd1933-X'1E'1X'7C'X'1F'aThe

bpaintedbbird,X'1F'cbybJerzybKosi

nski.X'1E'ØbX'1F'aNewbYork,X'1F'bTheb

ModernbLibrary,X'1F'c[1970,bc1965

]X'1E'bbX'1F'a234bp.X'1F'c22bcm.X'1E'bb

X'1F'a127299X'1D'
```

Main Entry

The concept of *main entry*, which is an authority file question, is somewhat different. If the data are converted according to international standards, then the use of those data can take two different routes. Each record can be kept intact as a unit or various elements can be split off, kept in different files, and linked back to the basic descriptive portion of the record. Take the record "Samuel Clemens," for example. In manual files it is essential that all materials by Samuel Clemens file together no matter how the name appears on a particular piece. This is accomplished by rules for entry; that is, change the form of the author's name to Clemens, or to the pseudonym Mark Twain, or to whatever the current rules state, and add cross-references from alternative forms to the one selected. It is also accomplished by placing each item under the author's name as it is on the title page and providing cross-references from each form to each of the other forms. Either method creates some problems in dealing with authors of a number of works.

When data are converted to a machine-readable form, and when the points controlled by an authority file are removed from the record and placed in a separate file, the entry has much more flexibility. There is, in this example, one entry in the authority file for "Clemens." That entry is linked to the descriptive portion of the bibliographic record so that each work by Clemens links up with the same entry point. Continuing, "Twain" can then be linked to "Clemens," which then links to all of the works by Clemens, no matter if the "main entry" in the original input was "Clemens" or "Twain" or any other form of the name in the authority file. The same can be true for variant forms of subject headings, series titles and the like.

Yet this does not mean that there is no requirement for authority files if one converts data. If one uses "Clemens." in one case and "Clemens" in another case for the conversion, then later there will be a software requirement to include both forms in order for the two to link together. If one uses a first initial one time and the full name another time, then the software used will have to bring both forms together. In using *Science Citation Index,* for example, to find all publications produced at one university, one must look under all forms of the name of that university. A short examination of a file output from a data base that does not use an authority file will be highly instructive concerning the need for authorities in machine-converted bibliographic data.

Thus, while the concept of main entry may be obsolete, the concept of authorities is not. All of the data will be available at any entry point and various forms of the entry point can be linked together, but there must be a controlled form for entry or all of the relevant information will not be recovered. There also must be a standard method for entry of all data or those which are recovered will not display in a uniform format.

CIRCULATION AND INVENTORY CONTROL

A major component of an integrated system is a record, or an inventory of each physical item in the collection. At any given point in time, a fully developed inventory system can give the status of each item in the collection, whether it is in circulation, on the shelves, missing, etc. This can only happen, however, if there is a discrete record for each physical item entered, and only if certain data elements are present in the record—either in the physical record or linked to that record in much the same way that authorities were linked.

In addition to the standardized description of the item, there must be standardized location information. This information is not as well developed in most online bibliographic systems as is the description of the item itself. In the Online Computer Library Center (OCLC) system, for example, the field tagged as 049 is used both to provide information for the card production program and to provide a magnetic tape record of the exact location of the item. Thus a particular receiving catalog in a particular part of the library (such as the reference shelf list in Branch A) can be designated, and if the profile of the library is on file, the converted data containing the 049 information can be linked to that exact location.

Unfortunately, the 049 field is used for too many different activities. The 049 field provides location information and controls the card printing program at OCLC. It may be used to input data printed on particular cards, such as the call number of the same item held in a different location, with a different call number. (When libraries using different fields from those used by a main library attempt to incorporate their data on cards, they may use the 049 field.) In addition, many have used this field to input bar code item numbers that are related to individual pieces, so that those numbers can be linked to a certain bibliographic record. This attachment of a machine-readable label to the physical item and the linking of that label to its corresponding bibliographic record, also in machine-readable form, is essential for a fully automated inventory control system.

The 049 field was never designed for much of these data. In some cases with a run of a monographic serial, the 049 field could easily contain in excess of 1000 characters. Even with a well-thought-out definition of the data to be input into the 049 field there can be many difficulties. Without such a definition, the data that one converts are prime candidates for later reconversion.

Selection of Data Elements

The data elements to be selected for presentation to the user often constitute only a subset of all the information input. As will be repeated often in this text, it is an error to base the data conversion effort on the first determination of the data elements that one may wish to retrieve. When in doubt, load the full record. This technique provides maximum flexibility for later system enhancement or modification.

On the other hand, one may very well select a subset of data elements for presentation to the user. Catalog use studies have shown that not many users require a full description of an item. Unfortunately, this has been translated into a desire not to provide those data to the system. When all data were entered manually, it made economic sense to design the input around the output required immediately. However, now that data conversion often means identifying a full bibliographic record from an abbreviated search key and then copying that full record into a user's bibliographic file, while keeping the record in machine-readable form, that method is obsolete.

In writing the specifications for the output requirements of any type of circulation or inventory system it is useful to select only a subset of the data that makes sense to the user. The unsophisticated user may need only the author, title and date of the material. The librarian helping him may require a more extensive record. The acquisitions librarian checking for duplication may need edition information, while the cataloger may require the full record. The automated inventory control system that data conversion makes possible may well be able to specify levels of information to be displayed. It is in the definition of those levels that catalog use studies can be valuable.

In the provision of the original data, however, it is an utmost necessity that the full national standard record be captured or developed. Without all of the data elements, including fixed field data, filing indicators, tags and complete description, there can be no new capabilities for the output beyond that first considered. Computer Output Microform (COM) catalogs may have frame after frame of titles beginning with *A* or *An* or *The* because nonfiling indicators were not present at the time of cataloging. The short title circulation system conversion of the early and mid-1970s is also limited. It is clear that the complete record, including both descriptive information and instructions to the computer, is essential if the data base is to develop first, second and third generation systems without a requirement for reconversion. Early in data conversion this lesson was not widely known and it resulted in a lot of wasted effort.

The Patron Identification File

Bibliographic conversion and data conversion in libraries are not interchangeable concepts. A file that is often forgotten in planning the conversion effort is the patron identification file. Unlike the bibliographic file that can be copied from an extensive and standard data base, often through any number of sources (see below), the patron file has few standards. In many academic libraries, in some school libraries and in some special libraries, a machine-readable patron file exists already. For example, a university registrar may have a file of faculty, staff and students which is used for all purposes from transcripts to payroll and tuition billings. While it is often possible to obtain a machine-readable tape of this file for initial loading in an inventory control system, academic librarians, from their manual systems, often have the best idea of current student addresses. The institution file is often far behind the daily changes that students make in living arrangements.

A school district may have a little better control of the current addresses of its students and other patrons but there is less of a chance that these data exist in a machine-readable format. A special library may have a file of employees but it often has confidential data, which makes it difficult to obtain even for in-house use.

Public libraries often face the largest task of patron registration and development of a machine-readable data base representing those individuals. There are often no other files to draw upon and even more confidentiality questions to consider.

No matter what the source of the initial data, the patron data have been designed, probably, for any purpose except that required for the library. Unless the library's needs are important to the institution, data elements necessary for circulation and inventory control systems may not be made available to the library in a usable form. Unlike national standard bibliographic data, the machine-readable tape provided to the library by some other agency, in the case of the public library, or by another part of the parent institution, in the case of other types of libraries, may not be well documented and can be the most difficult data to load in the library's system.

In almost every case the library will need to face a large one-time data conversion or data modification effort for its patron data. It behooves the library to take as much care in the development of the data for this file as it takes for the bibliographic file. Further, the library will also have to be concerned with the development of local standards for the design of the data elements and for the production of information. It will have to make provision for ongoing immediate entry of new patron data from well-designed input documents that fit the local situation. Unlike bibliographic data, which libraries are most willing to share with other libraries, these patron data may be confidential and care must be taken not to invade individuals' privacy.

Unlike bibliographic data entry, patron data entry may be a much larger continuing task than the description of the items owned. A small academic library may acquire only a few thousand new items per year but it could easily have a thousand patron additions, deletions and changes to contend with, all within the first week of the new semester. In sum, the area of patron identification is poorly designed compared with the bibliographic record and yet is often the one which requires the most continuing maintenance.

The identification of the item bibliographically and the patron biographically, both in machine-readable form, is not the entire task, however. The item itself must be linked to its machine-readable record and the patron must have an identification card to present when using the system.

Labeling

An item of library material is often identified by a machine-readable label. Such a simple sentence, however, does not describe a simple task. Although the American National Standards Institute (ANSI) Z39 Subcommittee SC V, "Standard Identification Numbers for Libraries, Library Items, and Library Patrons," has initiated the development of a national standard machine-readable label, there is as yet no standard. Should a library use a label that works with an optical character reader (OCR)? Should it, instead, use a bar code (of which there is more than one format now available)? Or should it hedge its bets by providing a more expensive label that provides for the use of either?

Moreover, should this label be placed in the material so that it can be read when a charge-out card or other representation of the due date is put in the item, or should the label be on the outside so that it can facilitate a later library inventory? If the label is on the outside, should a standard placement of the label be adopted? How will the label be protected from wear, mutilation and other damage?

There are still other considerations. What type of number should be encoded on the label? Should it be a number which has some specific significance or a number that is randomly or sequentially assigned, such as a key to the call number? How will the number be formatted so that it can be identified as an item label rather than as a patron label? What code should be on the label so that the material of one library can be distinguished from material belonging to another library?

How then will the bar code number be linked to the bibliographic record? While this might seem a relatively simple question, consider the labeling of a monographic series that could have more than 100 separate volumes, all described in a single bibliographic record.

14 DATA CONVERSION

In addition, should a link be made to the paper records that might have represented the item bibliographically prior to the data conversion? Many forward-looking libraries have used the techniques described below.

First they selected a label that combined both OCR and bar code capabilities. This has the advantage of making the bar code readable by the operator in case the input device fails and the number must be entered manually.

Although no standards exist now for library use of bar codes, the large number of bar codes provided for use by the CL Systems, Inc. (CLSI) circulation systems already in place have made the format of those labels a de facto standard. (See Figure 1.5.) The labels permit using a light pen beginning at either end of the label. The first code that is provided after the identification of the beginning and end of the label distinguishes between patrons and items. The next group of numbers is a library identification number. As is immediately obvious, there are not enough numbers available to provide a unique number for every library. The next group of numbers represents a sequential or random number which, through linking to the bibliographic record, identifies a specific item.

Figure 1.5 A Typical Bar Code

These item numbers are then linked to the bibliographic record either at the time of data conversion or later, through the circulation system. In many cases the links are made in the bibliographic record through such fields as the OCLC field 049. As was noted above, however, this field was never designed for this task and in the case of the monographic serial, 049 fields in excess of 1000 characters are possible.

Linking a machine-readable label from a physical item to its machine-readable bibliographic description is one of the weakest parts of the entire conversion process. It is not well defined, there are no national standards to support it, and it is often done in a way fraught with data entry error. Yet it is absolutely required if the bibliographic data conversion effort is to work. If there is one area that requires work before library data conversion can be effected it is this task, but because so much conversion of this type has already taken place it is probably too late for many libraries.

ACQUISITIONS AND IN-PROCESS

As noted above, the data base being developed needs to serve all library functions at least as well as the manual system that it will be replacing. In a number of organizations, materials that are somewhere in the acquisitions process may be the most important items of the collection. There are a number of studies indicating that the useful life of an item can be quite short, and it is not inconceivable that a large portion of this useful life can be spent attempting to reach the shelf.

Add to this fact the ideas that a library may wish to control duplication and that data should be converted only once to machine-readable form, and it becomes obvious that new data entry should be done at the earliest possible point in the acquisitions procedure. Unfortunately, information from prepublication sources, publishers and word of mouth may be somewhat faulty. While the title is often correct, most of the other bibliographic elements may be wrong. The establishment of the author/main entry, along with much of the descriptive information, can change between an announcement and publication.

The Acquisitions Record

In some ways it makes excellent sense to use the acquisitions record as a base for the later catalog record. The fact that the item is on order is known immediately and information about it can be retrieved. Through a verification process using a large machine-readable file, some inaccuracies and duplications can be identified. Comparison of the verified title with the current holdings can identify duplicates otherwise undetectable. Data conversion to support acquisitions also makes possible online order transmission. This can be a cooperative process involving a library, a vendor and a bibliographic utility such as Washington Library Network (WLN) or University of Toronto Library Automated Systems (UTLAS).

By appending a temporary holding or status code to the material, it can be tracked down within the technical processing department, after it arrives. Prior to that arrival, one can analyze vendor performance based on number of days to ship, number of items back-ordered, number of items missent, etc. After arrival, similar performance measures can be applied to technical processing operations.

As the suggested price, actual price, proposed discount, actual discount, etc. can be added to the record for the item, one can track expenses against various funds and in support of various audiences. Those data become most useful near the end of the fiscal year, when one wishes to maximize the material purchasing resources. Encumbrances, expenditures, vendor and library performance, physical location of the material, and elimination of duplication can all become part of the individual record of the item, as well as of the collective information.

This essential information, through enhancement, can be connected with an accounting system which can go as far as to calculate foreign currency conversions. However, it can become a burden if new information available when the item is received requires an extraordinary number of changes in the bibliographical description.

Upgrading the Record

From the point of view of data conversion, two questions must be answered: (1) Can data elements be extracted which provide enough of a description to minimize duplication but which maximize accounting and temporary location control? (2) Can the bibliographic elements that form the base of this system be exchanged or upgraded when the item is cataloged? The essential goal of avoiding reconversion must be kept in mind. The desirable record will permit discrimination among items, will permit the attachment of temporary location and accounting data, and can be upgraded through expansion rather than through replacement.

Extraction of data from another data base is more successful than the original keying of data. The library should develop a matching algorithm, which might be composed of the title up to the subtitle, the date and any standard number associated with the material. If these elements match those in a larger data base, then the record might be extracted at the time of the acquisition decision. If they do not, then the record in skeletal form might be added to the library's data base by original input and might be upgraded later in the cataloging process.

An individual library can modify its matching rules so as to provide for the minimum keying of data while developing an accurate data base.

SERIALS CONTROL

Complexity provides the impetus for a number of activities, including automation. Serials fit the definition of complexity more than any other class of library material. A single serial issue proceeds through the same life cycle of consideration, acquisition, cataloging, circulation and potential discard as does any other item but the task does not end there. (See the more detailed discussion of serials in Chapter 4.)

The acquisition of a serial item ordinarily means that additional pieces are to come without further orders. Those pieces can arrive in any order; they can be missed or delayed or never published. The serial will probably change some element of its bibliographic description over its life. The potential to split, merge, cease and/or skip necessitates complex acquisitions procedures, as well as detailed bibliographic and holdings information. These needs, along with the need to record the acquisition sources (purchase, gift, or deposit) and binding requirements, make serials automation advantageous. If one looks at the amount of funds and labor spent on serials, it becomes obvious that they warrant special consideration.

But it is easy to make a mistake with serials data. Planning, quality control, adherence to national standards and work with a dynamic, nationally connected data base are essential in serials work.

As noted in Chapter 4, automation of serials will be useful in acquisitions (both subscription placement and renewal) check-in and claims, and in binding. The machine-readable data, if managed properly, will support institutional and regional collection development. Those same data will provide input for union listing and will be the basis for significant resource-sharing activities.

Serials as a format of materials require library detail and expense. Their complexity and potential for data interchange necessitate the use of standards to communicate information about them.

All the rules of data conversion apply to serials. Automation for serials is more complex than for any library material, but the payoff can be the greatest. As with other aspects of data conversion, once the data to support serials control functions are machine readable, many by-products are also possible. Examples of by-products are analyses of vendor performance, organization of subscription information by account or fund number or by location or expiration date, and analyses of price increases. Many other manipulations of the serials control data can provide valuable information for library management.

RESOURCE SHARING

Much of the foregoing discussion implies resource sharing of one type or another. The inventory control system, particularly when connected with the circulation system, certainly makes it feasible for individual users to share the same collection. The acquisitions and in-process system certainly adds value to the collection resource by making it possible to find an item hidden away somewhere in the pipeline to the shelf. In the broad sense, all of these activities are a part of resource sharing. Traditionally, however, resource sharing means permitting other independent organizations to share in the use of a collection.

In times of limited resources it becomes difficult to think of independent, stand-alone library collections. A collection is redefined as the holdings of an entire region. This region is limited geographically only by transportation capability, which permits the movement of individual items from one location to another and by communications capability, which permits an individual user to know where a specific item is located. Given that the individual libraries within the region have worked out reciprocal agreements about borrowing (either interinstitutionally on interlibrary loan or lending directly to the user in some sort of reciprocal program), the concept of the collection can expand immediately from one institution to all of the holdings of a linked group of institutions.

The Electronic Union Catalog

Fifty years ago the management tool that was necessary to make such an arrangement operate was the union catalog. That concept has not changed today. What has changed is the way that the information in the union catalog can be manipulated, presented and used. Once in a national standard machine-readable format, the information describing the collection in one institution can be merged with data about many other institutions to form an *electronic* union catalog. This electronic catalog can simply identify items in each of the individual institutions.

However, complex catalogs, working with online circulation systems, inventory control systems and acquisition and in-process systems, can do much more. They can provide passive information about the status of any individual item in any individual library. They can also provide interactive capability, which allows any authorized user anywhere the opportunity to capture, hold, redirect and receive an item at any other location.

The idea might take some getting used to, but the technological capability now exists to distribute a single collection among several individual institutions under the control of an online, interactive, total management information system.

The key to all of that capability or to any part of it is data conversion. A well-planned data conversion process makes it possible for individuals converting data at several different locations to merge their information into a useful product. This is not as simple as it might first appear. The in-house uses of converted data, as described in this chapter, certainly increase the potential usefulness of the library. However, the interchange and merging of this information with collection description information from other institutions requires most careful planning and execution.

Value of the Electronic Catalog

Yet once this electronic union catalog is made available in either an online or a COM catalog—or, indeed, in a group of card-based catalogs—the capabilities of this collection of information far outweigh all of the effort necessary to build it. In this total resource-sharing environment, anything possible within a single institution becomes possible within the collective of cooperating institutions. The system, based on the data conversion that links the cooperating libraries, can be used for regional collection development, and to transmit requests that items at one location be sent to another. In essence, it can be used to maximize the single most valuable asset of any of the libraries: the collection.

MANAGEMENT INFORMATION

An online, integrated library system, based on the conversion of a full set of library data elements, provides the library manager with a powerful tool. As should be evident from the discussion above, it permits the location, control and use of the collection. It also permits the interchange of information among libraries, thus increasing the range and scope of the collection without a corresponding incremental cost. But the descriptive information also provides a different asset: a management information data base that describes the collection as a whole.

Consider, for example, the need in an academic library to understand how much of the collection supports a particular portion of the curriculum. For years library managers have measured portions of the shelflist to identify the number of items in a particular classification, which can then be related to certain portions of the curriculum. In the same way, the public library has examined its circulation to see, for example, how many persons in an individual township or census track or other geopolitical unit use certain items.

In almost every case imaginable, what is missing is cross-tabulation. It is one thing to know that a certain number of people in a certain census track check out a certain number of books. It is another thing to match characteristics of that population with characteristics of the books they check out. It is one thing to say at a city council meeting that Township X used 10% more items than they did a year ago, and it is another thing to say that the people associated with small businesses in Township X used items in the social sciences with imprints in the current year at a level 10% above a corresponding period a year ago.

The library never has been able to present anything except the rawest unanalyzed figures. The best it could say was that circulation was up. The very sophisticated public libraries might have been able to say circulation was up in a particular geographical or political unit. This does not have as much impact as being able to say that circulation is up and is contributing to the local economic efforts of the citizens, who in the end support that public library and its funder.

In an academic library it is one thing to say that 10% of the collection is related to the history department, and it is another thing to say that undergraduate students in history have used that extensive collection, but are now suffering because the average age by imprint year of the collection has increased over the past two years because of lack of acquisitions support.

In essence, data conversion efforts in the library permit, probably for the first time, an in-depth and accurate analysis of the interactions between the entire range of users and the entire range of the collection. Use measures of this type have been developed recently by the American Library Association, the National Center for Education Statistics and the American National Standards Institute. All of the systems, however, are greatly enhanced by manipulation of data elements in the records that describe the patrons, the collection and the overall financial resources available. In practical terms, that manipulation which provides new management information can only be done after a comprehensive data conversion effort has been completed. It is not the purpose of this text to describe that management information in detail, but to illustrate that data conversion in libraries serves much broader uses than that of providing catalog information.

SUMMARY

This chapter has focused on the new possibilities not available in a manual environment. As suggested above, data conversion is required for the development of integrated relationships both of one library to another and of one library system to another. Data conversion aids the traditional processes of circulation, cataloging, acquisitions and interlibrary loan but, equally important, it offers totally new capabilities. For the first time, the library can have a management information system which describes the most expensive portion of the library assets, the collection. That description can locate the inventory from the time that it is first ordered until it is discarded. That location, in turn, provides the ability to measure the performance of several in-library operations and outside library support operations.

Thus data conversion also provides, probably for the first time, access to a much wider universe—one that includes the collective resources of several independent units. Now the philosophy that gave rise to large-scale union catalogs can be put into practice. True resource sharing requires agreements among the individual institutions, which data conversion cannot affect, and it requires the ability to carry out these agreements, which data conversion can make possible.

All of this will remain at the philosophical level, however, unless the data conversion is well planned, complete and standardized. Chapters 2 and 3 describe the planning required for this data conversion effort; Chapter 4 discusses special considerations in data conversion. Without the kind of detailed planning effort outlined here, the library may need to reconvert the data when an in-house sub-unit finds that central information is missing and/or when the library attempts to share or merge its data with those of another organization. Chapter 5 describes the various methods of data conversion and reviews the requirements for each. Problems encountered in actual data conversion projects and approaches to be avoided are the subject of Chapter 6. Chapter 7 presents a brief summary of data conversion trends. Appendixes A, B and C, compiled by Elaine Rast of Northern Illinois University, present a wealth of information on libraries involved in data conversion efforts, consultants on data conversion and data conversion equipment vendors.

2
Planning for Data Conversion: Project Analysis

A library may take three principal approaches to a data conversion project. They are:

1. The library will do a data conversion project of a specified magnitude. The problem is not whether or not to do it, or how much to do, but rather how best to accomplish it.

2. There will be a data conversion project but the scope is not decided yet. The problem is to determine how much should be done and how best to accomplish it.

3. Should there be a data conversion effort at this time? If the answer is yes, the library then must determine how much to convert and how best to accomplish the conversion.

THE INITIAL ANALYSIS PROCESS

Several basic steps in the initial analysis and decision-making process for a data conversion project should be followed. These are:

1. Establish the library's goals and objectives for a conversion effort, either retrospective or prospective.

2. Describe the existing conditions, including the data that could be converted (determining the source of the data).[1]

3. Identify needs for staff or vendor to accomplish the conversion.

4. Make local decisions on standards and formats.

5. Consider available resources.

6. Evaluate the data and make a final decision.

A description of each of the basic components in the initial analysis phase follows.

ESTABLISH GOALS AND OBJECTIVES

Any data conversion project is a major undertaking with both short- and long-term implications. When a library is considering a conversion effort, either retrospective or ongoing, it must make some basic decisions.

If the library administration has decided to put some or all of its records into machine-readable form in order to have a computer-based system, it must decide what data elements should be included and to what format they should be converted. For bibliographic data, the MARC format has become widely accepted. MARC was developed by the Library of Congress and allows for very specific identification of the various data elements as well as for completeness of the bibliographic information. Not all conversion efforts have chosen or will choose to select the MARC format for all possible data elements.

Initial decisions on format and completeness affect both short- and long-term uses of the data, as well as the speed with which conversion can be accomplished. As the decisions are being made, a library should take the advice of Marcum and Boss to "keep in mind that the data base that is being built will not only last as long as the computer system but for several generations of computer systems."[2] That is, a machine-readable data base can be expected to have a very long time of usefulness. Thus, it seems wise to base conversion on full records, unless there are overwhelming constraints against that alternative.

The library must carefully define what it expects to accomplish once it has converted its records. It must know its first application (perhaps circulation or acquisitions), and it must identify eventual applications (for example: an online catalog capable of supporting subject searching; the capacity to support analysis of the growth and use of the collection to aid management decision making; or production of selected bibliographies on demand).

Even if a library does not foresee the need for a full bibliographic record, it should be very careful to provide the capacity for the easy expansion of its data at a later time. This means that the data elements selected should be converted to a format in which they are readily distinguishable. At least one data element should be selected that will lend itself to matching against another machine-readable data base.

By including a specific data element which is unique to the item, not the library, future flexibility can be assured, even though data elements converted initially may be limited. Examples of this type of search key are the Library of Congress Card Number (LCCN), the International Standard Book Number (ISBN), and the International Standard Serial Number (ISSN). The ISSN, however, can be assigned to both hard copy titles and microfiche or microfilm. Therefore, it can be used partially, but not exclusively, to match records. However, as noted by Radke and Montgomery, the ISSN can be valuable as one element in matching records by machine.[3]

A library's goals and objectives may lead to one set of conversion criteria for some or all of its retrospective materials and a different set for its current and future materials. This type of situation can result when a balance is sought between the ideal and the practical. For example, a library may want an online catalog as part of an integrated system. In that case, ideally, the catalog would have a full record for everything. But economic circumstances may dictate something less. Therefore, in order to support circulation as one component of an integrated system, brief records may be converted for some of the titles in the collection. The University of Illinois Library at Urbana-Champaign, for example, has some full bibliographic records as a result of cataloging on OCLC, and some brief bibliographic records with their detailed holdings, for the remainder of its collection, in order to support its online circulation system.[4]

DESCRIBE EXISTING CONDITIONS

Before any firm decisions can be made for a data conversion project, it is necessary to describe the present situation and clearly describe and quantify the existing data. Without knowing the number of records under consideration and the number of data elements contained in those records, it is impossible to determine costs and resources required, or to evaluate alternative conversion approaches.

The library must first establish the number of separate files that might be considered for conversion. It must then answer the following questions for each separate file:

1. How many records are in the file?

2. What are the data elements in the records?

3. For what purpose(s) is the file used?

4. How is the file maintained?

5. How many new records and/or updates are added/changed in the file on a daily, weekly, monthly or annual basis?

6. How often is the file accessed?

7. Is part or all of the information in any single file duplicated in one or more other files?

8. Are some or all of the records inactive or rarely consulted?

9. Do the data elements conform to specific standards? If so, what are the standards and have they varied over a period of time? If not, what types of variations are present in the data?

Existing files may need to be sampled in order to answer the above questions. The files in question may be card catalogs, serial records, documents inventories or on-order and in-process files. All of those, plus others, are likely candidates for conversion to machine-readable form. (Although this discussion of conversion emphasizes the bibliographic/catalog records, the steps in conversion planning apply to all library files that might be considered for conversion to machine-readable form.)

Numerous techniques exist for the process of sampling a given file. A shelflist, as defined by Carter, is the most common bibliographic file selected for data conversion.[5] Butler, Aveney and Scholz provide instructions for "choosing a random sample from a shelflist."[6] They point out that the initial consideration in determining the size of the sample is the number of volumes in the collection that are represented in the catalog. For example, a university catalog with a shelflist of 800 to 900 trays, having 800 to 900 cards per tray, would require a sample of only one or two cards per tray. Collections of 500,000 volumes or fewer require two or three cards per tray.

In general, the smaller the file, the higher the portion of it that must be checked in order to have a statistically reliable sample. If a library is sampling multiple files in multiple locations, the portion of a file checked may vary, depending on the size of the individual file.

Butler, Aveney and Scholz provided a page divided into 10 "rulers."[7] Each ruler has five points, numbered 1 through 5. The numbers appear in different intervals and sequences on the 10 rulers. By cutting a copy of the page into 10 sections, numbered 0 to 9, 10 rulers are created. These can be copied multiple times and numbered 10-19, 20-29, 30-39, or one for each drawer in the shelflist. By then using the numbers on each ruler, the necessary number of cards can be selected from each tray and photocopies can be made to provide an analyzable sample of the shelflist or other file.

Using the above technique, or an even simpler one of the librarian's choice, a file can be analyzed and described in sufficient detail to enable necessary decisions to be made. These include establishing specifications for conversion and deciding whether the conversion should be done in-house or contracted for with a vendor. If the library decides to use a vendor, a description of the file must be submitted to the vendor so he can prepare cost estimates and present a bid.

Either the library staff or a vendor is likely to use an outside data base, such as those maintained by OCLC, Research Libraries Information Network (RLIN) or the MARC records distributed by the Library of Congress as the source data base for the conversion. Therefore, many samples are compared against one of those data bases and evaluated in terms of its records. Frequently considered categories for sampling records in a shelflist are:

1. Records in the shelflist that match records in the source data base exactly. This category sometimes includes records that differ only in call number.

2. Records in the shelflist that differ from the records in the source data base in a way that does not require editing. In other words, the existing machine-readable record can be accepted.

3. Records in the shelflist that differ from the records in the source data base and which require editing of the source data base records in order to make them acceptable.

4. Records that are not in the source data base and require total keying and entry into machine-readable form.

A conversion sample often takes into account the dates of publication found in the bibliographic records for the titles in the shelflist. This is because the more recent the date of publication, the higher the percentage of materials that are located in the source data bases. Therefore, publication date may be used as a criterion in deciding what portion of a file to convert, at least initially.

Another way in which a file can be described that affects conversion decisions is the percentage of foreign-language materials. In general, foreign-language materials are more complex than English-language materials to put into an automated system. Therefore, the number of foreign-language items in a particular file, either present or future, can affect conversion decisions, as well as other related decisions. These include decisions concerning hardware and software used both for input and output. Terminals and printers might be examined for their capacity to handle diacritics, and machine-readable products such as computer output microform (COM) might be considered.

IDENTIFY STAFF/VENDOR NEEDS

At an early stage, a library manager must identify the alternative methods of handling data conversion, and consider who will do the actual work, both retrospective and ongoing. Ordinarily, ongoing data conversion should become an integral part of the library's work flow; existing positions should be restructured, if necessary, to include input to an automated system as a regular routine.

There are several methods available to handle one-time retrospective conversion efforts. The common alternatives are:

1. Use existing library staff to accomplish the conversion in-house.

2. Do the conversion in-house but with extra staff hired specifically for the conversion project.

3. Have it done outside by a vendor.

4. Use a combination of any of the three basic methods.

The last often becomes the fact in real life, when utilization of an outside conversion service is selected.

Each of the approaches to a conversion effort has advantages and disadvantages.

Each general method presents options in organizing the work. The options are briefly summarized here to assist in identifying alternatives—an essential part of the planning process. They are discussed more fully in Chapters 3 and 5. Library managers must analyze all options, in conjunction with the other variables, such as content of the file or files to be converted, goals of automating and resources available.

In-house with Existing Staff

Accomplishing the conversion in-house with existing staff has the advantage of using trained and knowledgeable people to do the work. However, if regular work is stopped, then a backlog will build up. If conversion is done on a scheduled part-time or as-time-permits basis, it is very likely to be an excessively lengthy and drawn-out process, which may be detrimental to both the current work and the conversion project. If it is done only on an as-time-permits basis, the conversion may never be finished, especially in a large library doing an extensive conversion. In general, it is unlikely that many libraries have staff with much spare time.

In-house with Special Staff

To accomplish the conversion in-house but with special project staff requires other considerations. Extra desks, chairs and other furniture or equipment may be required or the library may need to establish a second shift if basic equipment must be shared. This is particularly true for conversions based on source data bases, such as OCLC or RLIN, where terminal time may be at a premium.

The advantage of in-house conversion, even with separate staff, is that the files being converted remain close at hand for both the project and regular work. In-house conversion also facilitates related efforts such as inventory of the collection and bar coding. Even if a separate project staff is retained, it is normally possible to provide for some overlap with the most expert or knowledgeable regular staff. Therefore, problems encountered can be resolved fairly rapidly.

Using Vendor Services

Conversion using a vendor's services can be most efficiently accomplished in two basic ways. A common method is for the library to send some or all of its file(s) out to a vendor, usually in small batches at regular intervals. Sometimes the library will choose to make a copy of its records before it sends them out. An alternative approach is to contract with a conversion agency that will send its employees to the library for on-site conversion. Often, a conversion effort undertaken with a commercial agency will require some additional effort by the library staff. For example, if no matching record is found in a source data base, the library's records may be returned for original entry into the source data base, such as OCLC, or directly into the local system.

The method or combination of methods selected for any specific situation will depend on analysis of the possible conversion methods, taking into account the other components of the conversion project. These include: (a) the size and nature of file(s) to be converted; (b) the standards according to which the conversion will be accomplished; (c) the project's overall goals and objectives; and (d) the resources available. It is important to emphasize that in the planning process, decisions concerning any one element of the conversion process should not be made in isolation from the other elements.

MAKE LOCAL DECISIONS ON STANDARDS AND FORMATS

Most conversion projects undertaken in the 1980s will involve the use of a major source data base with records in nationally accepted standards and formats. Even the essentially local system at the Pennsylvania State University libraries uses the MARC tapes along with local input.[8] All machine-readable records created by Penn State are also in accordance with national standards and formats. This standardization is critical to the future ability to share and exchange records with other institutions, networks or utilities.

In 1981 Richard De Gennaro provided a look at libraries and networks as they can be expected to continue to evolve in the 1980s.[9] By their nature, computer-based systems have more capabilities than comparable manual systems, they are more expensive, and they impose higher standards both for cataloging and for the maintenance of the catalog in machine-readable format.

Thus, any data conversion project must deal with the question of standards as one of the fundamental factors on which to base decisions. Because of the emphasis on national standards, there is a growing tendency for records generated in a conversion project to be as complete as possible and for the data elements in the records to be current and up to date. In 1979 the Retrospective Conversion Task Force of the OCLC Internetwork Quality Control Council surveyed 446 libraries on the possibility of having separate standards for quality and/or quantity of the data input in a retrospective conversion project.[10] The large majority of respondents indicated a strong preference for having the same standards for current cataloging and retrospective conversion. Johnson suggests that those requirements will in and of themselves require that more conversion projects be done by library staff rather than by commercial vendors.[11]

While short-term considerations such as the speed and economy with which conversion can be accomplished lure decision makers into considerations of expediency, long-term benefits and potential applications mitigate in favor of both completeness and accuracy. Metz summarized the limitations of anything less than full standard records as a part of an integrated system. They include "redundant data, inconsistencies, the expense of parallel systems, and very limited future options."[12]

Existing Standards

What standards exist as factors in the conversion of bibliographic records? They include the MARC format for the communication of bibliographic data; cataloging rules, with the second edition of the *Anglo-American Cataloguing Rules* (*AACR2*) as the current standard; and subject heading standards.[13] The last may vary by type of library, particularly in medical libraries or small public and school libraries. For the large majority of libraries, however, the *Library of Congress Subject Headings* is the accepted standard. In classification, the Library of Congress and Dewey Decimal Classification systems are widely accepted standards.[14]

There is no standard for the machine communication of holdings data. Carter, Pierce and others have pointed out this omission.[15,16] Fortunately, work in this area is in progress.[17] There is one standard available for the content of summary holdings data for serials, but in the book field, there is no standard for either content or communication of holdings data. There is a crucial need for both.

The widespread adoption of *AACR2* has complicated retrospective conversion decision making. This will be discussed in more detail in Chapter 4. However, it is important to note here that the extent to which *AACR2* becomes a factor in conversion is in part related to which bibliographic utility, if any, is serving as a source data base. This is because adoption of *AACR2* as a standard varies from one bibliographic utility to another. A library using OCLC as its source data base will find its conversion process radically affected by OCLC and its *AACR2* policies in at least two ways.

The first factor is that OCLC did a machine conversion to *AACR2* form, called "flip," of at least one name heading in 39% of records in its online data base.[18] This means that a library's catalog record for a title may contain a pre-*AACR2* form of name. A library must then decide which form of name to use. If the library chooses to use the *AACR2* form for its new machine record (as it should), it must make a second decision on whether or not to change existing manual records.

Second, and perhaps even more significant to a large library that might find 10% to 15% or more of its titles not in the data base, is the fact that OCLC requires that all new titles input into its online data base be in accordance with *AACR2*. In most cases, this will require looking at the physical piece in order to formulate a complete cataloging record. Therefore, a vendor cannot effectively do the original input.

The need to use *AACR2* for new input might influence the extent of a retrospective conversion effort. For example, a library that found that 20% of its titles with an imprint date before 1960 require original input, but only 5% of those from 1960 forward are not in the source data base, might decide to convert backward only to 1960. The other side of that approach, however, is that the records not found in the source data base would be a major contribution to national and international bibliographic control of library resources.

RLIN has not adopted *AACR2* as stringently as has OCLC. It did not do a machine "flip" of the headings found in its online records. Nor does RLIN require strict *AACR2* adherence for conversion projects when entering new records into the data base. In part, this is because RLIN anticipates that authority files will help make differences in form of names transparent to users of public access systems.

Both University of Toronto Automated Library Systems (UTLAS) and Washington Library Network (WLN) have online authority control. The WLN system has been known for its authority and quality control, as well as its search capabilities, since the introduction of its bibliographic subsystem in 1976.

Contributions of Authority Files

Authority files can serve as a means of evaluating the validity of headings in bibliographic records going into a data base. They can also be used to collocate groups of records where the same heading appears with different forms.[19] Both are important purposes. Machine-based systems cannot be searched properly if there are typographical errors in the search key part of an access point. Furthermore, the machine-based system has no facility for simple stand-alone cross references, which lead the patron to other forms of a name or subject. Instead, a patron can locate all related entries through a machine-based authority system. Many libraries look to this as an answer to the continuing problems of catalog maintenance, which appear regardless of the format of the catalog. In discussing consistency in retrospective conversion, Malinconico and Fasana caution that "on the whole, techniques to upgrade and render consistent a bibliographic file *after* conversion will not be as effective as those employed *during* the conversion process."[20]

The presence or absence of an authority file during a conversion project is one factor in choosing the standards to be employed. As was suggested above, if in doubt, it is better to take the time to bring records up to standard as they are converted. This is particularly true for forms of name headings, but it can also be true for subject headings. For example, if a library's old catalog records still have the heading "Spanish America" instead of "Latin America," it would probably be a disservice to convert the obsolete heading. In order to assist the patron in finding everything on a topic, librarians involved in conversion planning should attempt to facilitate collocation.

Conversion of Subject Headings

Recent research, funded by the Council on Library Resources, on public access of online catalogs indicates that in an online catalog, more than 50% of the searches are subject searches.[21] This clearly has an impact on conversion planning in at least two areas of consideration. One is the completeness of a bibliographic record that could be converted. In the early days of library automation, brief records were very popular and subject headings were often left out of the machine-readable record. This was particularly true when circulation was the first function selected for automation. Because we now know that online catalogs are used heavily for subject searching, it would be shortsighted to eliminate subject headings from the list of data elements to be converted.

The question now becomes, "To what standard should we convert subject headings?" Should subject headings in older records be converted to their current equivalents? Simply from the standpoint of time involved, it might be impractical in most cases to check every single subject heading in records with a particular date of cataloging. Perhaps there could be a list of commonly encountered changes, such as "Spanish America" to "Latin America" or "European War, 1914-1918" to "World War, 1914-1918." Where to draw the line in this regard is a problem.

Of course, not all subject searching in an online system will be done against the subject heading fields as such. In many systems the title, as well as other fields, can be used in subject searching, in which case both key-word and Boolean searching techniques can be employed. The greater capacities for subject searching in free text and Boolean searching suggest that it may not be necessary to give much concern to the subject headings. Nevertheless, the subject headings themselves are a vital access point, and a printed subject heading list may help patrons to establish terms to be used in a search. Further, an increased demand for subject searching overall suggests that care should be taken with subject entries.

Another possibility is to convert subject headings as they are found in a source data base and then to use a machine-readable subject authority file to make global subject heading changes, or to provide the user with all variant entries, regardless of the heading used in a search. (A global change is where one command to change one form of a name will change all occurrences of that name.) The need for machine-based authority files in local systems is widely recognized, although few have been provided. Indeed, as Govan observed, a lot of people discuss authority control, but often in the abstract.[22] It is frequently unclear whether most use of the term refers to name authority only, or to the whole range of name, series and subject authority.

Conversion of Authority Files

Many librarians do not fully understand authority control and its place in a conversion process or online system. They often disagree about whether it is necessary, and about possible different end uses of the data in the conversion. Thus authority control requires careful consideration in the planning process. Input from staff regarding probable use patterns of online files can be important.

Authority control decisions are important in both retrospective and prospective conversion. The process must include planning for maintenance of a library's bibliographic records. However, if changes to existing catalog records have been made only on cards, the machine-readable data base being built for new cataloging may not include maintenance updates. If the library has an authority file that can be converted to the automated system, the problem may work itself out. If, however, there are no early plans to convert the authority file to machine-readable form, unchanged catalog records may lead to serious problems in the future.

A decision should not be made automatically to skip shelflist records, just because they were made machine-readable previously. However, a partial solution may be an automated system that provides for the capacity, on a case-by-case basis, to make global changes. VTLAS, the system at Virginia Polytechnic Institute & State University, is a locally developed library system which has that capability.

Procedures for current activities should be identified, and maintenance of machine records should be incorporated into ongoing routines. If that is not feasible, planning must include the eventual maintenance of these records after they are loaded into a local, probably online, system. Conversion decisions with regard to authority control need to be made in terms of a known or probable automated system selection. They must also take into account what is possible and practical versus what might be ideal and/or theoretically available at some future point.

With the partial exception of a system like that at Virginia Polytechnic Institute, for those situations mentioned, the definition of an authority file as one generated from all names, series, and/or subjects occurring in the data, including variant name fields, is not adequate. This would provide a register of headings that occur but would not provide a complete syndetic reference structure to direct patrons to everything pertinent to one heading. However, as Gorman noted, the computer has the capability, with the right programming and a responsive machine-readable subject-heading list, to provide more links between subject headings than a normal authority file would provide.[23] Gorman also suggests that subject searches, even on broad terms, can be improved with qualification by date, by language and so on.

In the meantime, Govan suggests that if the major purpose of the conversion is to enter holdings into a network, regional or area catalog to serve as a finding tool for locations, such a reference structure may not be necessary.[24] Rather, authority control may be most important in individual libraries, where the user often approaches the catalog with a broad search rather than with a known item for which he or she wants a location.

The MARC Format

Associated with the question of standards for the actual content of the data is the question of formats to be used. The question often asked about a system is: "Is it MARC compatible?" What precisely is "MARC compatible"? Ordinarily a system is considered MARC compatible if it will accept input in MARC format, store internally each data element in a uniquely identifiable manner, and write a record in full MARC format. It is understood that for purposes of internal data manipulation any given system does not store data in MARC format. However, unless a system can recreate a full MARC record as output, it is not MARC compatible. "Full MARC record" connotes the presence of fixed fields, subfields and indicators of the variable fields, plus the full ALA character set including diacritics.

Conversion to a local system may or may not be to a MARC compatible format. Because other uses for the data are hard to foresee, it is recommended that consideration be given to choosing MARC compatible formats wherever possible. Even if some data elements are not converted, future options should be left open.

The question of format becomes a critical area in regard to nonbibliographic data. These include holdings data of all types for all formats of material; data normally associated with acquisitions systems, including accounting information; and circulation system data. A library must have in mind the purposes for which the data will be used. If data are for local use only—for example, fiscal information—a format designed for just one system is probably satisfactory. However, if data are to be shared or to be furnished to vendors for production of COM catalogs or similar products, it is important to have a format that is "standard" and readily transferable or intelligible.

As noted previously, work is in progress for a MARC communications format for holdings data of all types. This will address both physical and bibliographic pieces. The first is necessary for circulation/inventory systems; the second is needed in bibliographic control systems. Existing holdings standards, as compared to formats, address only bibliographic items. Because many conversion projects must provide a basis for circulation systems, the questions of the format for the communication of holdings data and a standard for the content of physical piece representation take a high priority. Exchange of data on item availability has implications for both interlibrary lending and collection development.[25]

CONSIDER AVAILABLE RESOURCES

No conversion effort, either retrospective or prospective, can be undertaken without adequate resources. These include bibliographic resources encompassing the local data, supporting sources, and a source data base, either from a bibliographic utility or a commercial vendor. Other resources essential to both one-time and ongoing conversion efforts are people, equipment, space, time and money. Careful evaluation of resources is necessary for the ultimate success of a conversion project. Each of the necessary resource components is discussed below.

Bibliographic Resources

A number of different bibliographic entities are grouped under the category of bibliographic resources. Basic to any conversion are the files to be converted because they constitute the fundamental resource. A sampling of the files, as described above, will indicate whether or not the data in local records are complete. Knowing whether or not a shelflist record can be used as is will affect the assessment of the adequacy of other available resources, particularly the human resources.

Another essential bibliographic resource is supporting files, to assist in quality control. Some of these, such as local authority files (name, series and/or subject), may themselves be candidates for conversion to machine-readable form. A library must take stock of its bibliographic tools, including those as basic as the *National Union Catalog*.

Besides printed tools or local files, access to online source bibliographic data bases must also be considered. For example, does a library have direct access to a bibliographic utility such as OCLC, RLIN, WLN (which has a retrospective conversion subsystem) or UTLAS? If so, to which? What percentage of its potentially convertible records are found in the utility's data base? And, of those found, what are the nature and magnitude of the differences in records for the same titles?

It is also necessary to establish the size and form of the files to be converted now and to determine how fast the files are being increased or otherwise modified. If any of the files are already machine readable, conversion to a different machine-readable format may be facilitated. It is necessary to understand the demands that will be placed on a library's resources both on a project basis and on an ongoing basis. Perhaps a library has resources to keep up with the current conversion of its files, but does not have or cannot get the resources to accomplish retrospective conversion. Again, conversion decisions and plans must be made by reviewing a number of different factors.

Human Resources

No conversion effort can take place without people. Are the human resources available within the library's own staff, or will it be necessary to secure outside help? This question applies to the planning and design of a conversion process as well as to the actual conversion of data. Staff availability must be measured in terms of both expertise and numbers of people. A library should question the abilities of its in-house staff to plan, organize and direct a conversion effort. These questions are more critical than that of staff availability. The nitty gritty can be learned through training and experience as the work proceeds. The organizational and managerial skills need to be present from the beginning of the project.

If the library does not have a staff member who can organize a conversion project, it may want to hire a consultant for this purpose. One or more outside consultants could be useful in a variety of roles. These include:

1. Description of the present situation;

2. Evaluation of existing resources, including the library's files;

3. Development and recommendation of a conversion plan;

4. Presentation of alternative plans, with no specific recommendation;

5. Design of the project;

6. Training of existing staff;

7. Review of progress of a project;

8. Preparation of Request For Proposal (RFP) or Request For Quotation (RFQ) to vendors;

9. Analysis of responses to RFPs or RFQs;

10. Review of a library's own planning and project design;

11. Recommendation for future capabilities as an extension of current or future conversion.

The library can identify consultants in a variety of ways. These include: checking reference sources listing consultants, responding to advertising by consultants, asking the network or other libraries with experience in similar projects for suggestions, and reviewing the literature to identify individuals with obvious experience and expertise. (Appendix B is a selected list of consultants.)

Staff required to do actual conversion must be determined. It is critical that this be done thoroughly, both because of the need for adequate staff to accomplish target goals in a stated period of time and because funding for staff is likely to be the most costly part of a proposal.[26] As with other aspects of initial planning and evaluating, this must be viewed in relation to other components of the process. Some questions to ask are:

1. Does existing staff have experience in data entry and/or conversion of data from manual to machine-readable form?

2. If not, can they be trained for this work?

3. Who will provide direct supervision?

4. Who will be responsible for quality control?

5. Does staff have individuals with those areas of expertise?

6. Who will coordinate the conversion project with existing, related library activities?

7. Is there enough staff to do a retrospective project on a crash basis or on a gradual basis?

8. How much of each individual's time will the project take?

9. Is there sufficient staff to handle the ongoing work associated with a conversion commitment?

10. Can conversion duties be substituted for other duties that will no longer be necessary?

11. If the desired data conversion is accomplished, can staff be reduced or reassigned to other areas?

12. If extra staff must be hired, how many would be required and what qualifications would they need?

13. How many and what hours should they work?

14. How can terminal time be scheduled to minimize fatigue and/or health hazards?

15. How can provision be made for interaction with regular staff?

Many of the answers to the questions under the heading "Human Resources" will relate to answers given in other areas, such as the scope of the project and the conversion criteria. For example, far fewer personnel will be required if the conversion process does not include bar coding each item and an accompanying inventory, prior to conversion, of the bibliographic record for any particular item. A good plan involves decisions on all the major options. Evaluation of resources is one important element in effective planning. As Wetherbee stated, "It is costly and inefficient to begin conversion without at least some quantitative idea of your resources and support for the duration of a special project."[27]

This same knowledge is also necessary for an ongoing process. Even if all the ongoing issues are not resolved initially, the library decision-maker must be aware of them and provide accordingly. Barkalow advised that staff is expensive and should be used wisely.[28] One way to accomplish this is by planning carefully, providing clear written instructions and always stressing accuracy. The last is very important despite the expense and the time and effort involved. A fast, sloppy conversion job may cause the library users to doubt the value of conversion and may frustrate the staff as well.

Equipment and Supplies

A conversion effort, at least if done in-house, requires equipment of one type or another. Before a library can decide how much and what kind of equipment is needed, it must determine whether the conversion effort that will be undertaken is one-time or ongoing. Equipment for either type of project encompasses a wide range of categories.

In order to accommodate new staff, additional floor space, furniture and supplies must usually be provided. In some cases, staff members may be able to share work stations. This will depend on the hours during which staff are scheduled to work and the extent to which there is overlap. If extra work stations or desks are required, the library must have sufficient space to accommodate them.

Hardware

The major equipment requirements, at least in terms of cost, are in the area of hardware. If conversion of bibliographic records is going to be accomplished via a bibliographic utility, the library manager may want to acquire extra cathode ray terminals (CRTs), especially for a large-scale effort projected over several years. (These terminals display information on a TV-like screen.) A library should take into account future uses for the terminals. For example, it may be possible to move them later to public service locations within the same institution or to make them available to other libraries. Terminals used in a dial access mode (which dial into the data base using a telephone, but do not have a full-time connection) are theoretically usable, but would be slow and impractical in a conversion project of any size. In buying terminals, or other equipment, it is also necessary to consider service fees that might be incurred.

If a library does not foresee a permanent need for terminals, it may be able to lease one or more terminals from another institution or network. Perhaps it might even barter use of a terminal for some other item or service. Another option is to rent time on a terminal at another location and send its staff to the terminal. This is one method to minimize equipment needs.

Entry of the data into the utility, editing the data and transfer of the data to the local institution for use may be accomplished in a number of ways, each of which requires equipment. The most conventional method for getting converted bibliographic data back to the library is by magnetic tapes. These can be obtained directly by the individual institution or by the network to which the library belongs. In the second case, the network might have the capability of stripping off records for the individual institution. Examples of networks with this capability in late 1982 are AMIGOS and the Pittsburgh Regional Library Center (PRLC). Storing tapes, then, should be part of overall library automation planning.

A "black box" interface between a utility terminal and the local system might be secured specifically for the conversion effort. The same is true of a microcomputer. Microcomputers can be important aids both in data entry and data editing, and one or more may be acquired as part of a conversion project. One project using a microcomputer is at the B.F. Jones Memorial Library in Beaver County, PA.

A library may combine data conversion with bar coding or putting optical character recognition (OCR) labels on items, whether the items are already in the collection or are being acquired. In that case it is necessary to plan for the equipment related to the labeling process. This can include the purchase of light pens, bar code and/or OCR labels, label-makers and related items.

Depending on the source of computer support for a conversion effort, the library may need to ask additional questions. If it does not have an in-house computer, will it have adequate time on the outside computer? Will available computer time be compatible with the library's schedule? If the computer is off-site, does it have remote data entry capability? Will it handle the work fast enough? Is the library likely to be preempted at critical times? (Some of these considerations will not be pertinent if a library chooses to have most or all of its conversion done by an outside vendor.)

Software

Software needs also come under the general heading of equipment and supplies. A conversion project may include an upgrading of data already in machine-readable form. Depending on the method used to input changes to existing records, some programming may be involved, which can be locally developed or a commercial software package. The Yale University library system has used a commercial software package to identify the correct records among duplicates in Yale's archive tape from OCLC.[29] North Carolina State University's D.H. Hill Library developed programming locally to handle maintenance of its machine-readable data base created from its OCLC archive tape.[30] By-products of this effort also included cataloging statistics, classified acquisitions lists and error reports.

Revising records on OCLC or RLIN and receiving duplicate records on an archive tape represent one approach to changing existing machine-readable records. In some cases, the data may be loaded into a local system and edited there. Or existing machine-readable records, such as brief records on punched circulation cards, might be machine matched by call number to get a fuller record. Any of these can require the development of software, which will mean some additional cost. Whether it is a direct extra cost or one that can be absorbed by a staff programmer, it is nonetheless a cost in money or in a staff person's time.

As with all elements that make up a conversion effort, equipment and supplies must be considered in relationship to the other components. Even the equipment necessary to photocopy manual files or to otherwise backup converted records cannot be overlooked.

Space

Before a library can add either equipment or staff for a conversion project, it must ascertain whether or not it has sufficient floor space. Many of the same questions generated in relation to equipment and staff are relevant here. If the conversion effort requires extra work stations, will there be enough floor space? Is space available for an adequate period of time? Is it convenient to regular staff and to the file(s) being converted? Must the library pay extra for it?

Time

Time can be a factor in several areas of planning. First, the library must know if there are any specific time constraints. Perhaps funding for the actual conversion, particularly retrospective or initial conversion, includes time restrictions. Perhaps special government funds must be expended in a particular time frame, or a grant has a definite time limit.

A second area of consideration with relation to time is staff and user toleration for the duration of a big project. Users should not be disappointed about the availability of a product or service, and staff should not be frustrated because a project seems endless. On the other hand, a large institution may have an ultimate goal of having 75% or more of its collection in machine-readable form, and might state at the outset that it plans a long-term project (perhaps as long as five or 10 years).

Determining the duration of a conversion project can only be done in the context of planning for staff, space and equipment. In addition, a retrospective data conversion project should not be looked at without considering the ongoing work of the library. None of these is easy to see, and so a chart or model unique to the library can be constructed. Such a model will also aid in the understanding of another key area of resources: money.

Financial Resources

Before any library commits itself to either retrospective or prospective data conversion, it should determine if it has or can obtain sufficient financial resources to support the conversion effort. In part this is an iterative process because once a library determines what it wants to do and establishes its available financial support, the library managers may find that the two are incompatible. It is advisable to develop complete conversion plans based on the library's ultimate goals, and then attempt to get all the necessary funds. A project can always be scaled down later to match the fiscal reality. Establishing a limited

38 DATA CONVERSION

target initially may result in less funding than might have been available if higher goals had been set.

Evaluating Costs

The library considering conversion must answer these questions: What will costs be if conversion is done in-house versus by a vendor? What will some combination of the two cost? If an in-house project is planned, the following costs must be identified and calculated: type and number of staff, equipment needs (whether purchased or leased), supplies, fixed costs of a bibliographic utility, conversion costs through a utility, and overhead costs, if assumed by the library staff.

In considering the costs of introduction of the Library Computer System (LCS) to a library in Illinois, McGregor listed data conversion as the biggest initial outlay.[31] In the case of that library, 21 cents per title was provided by the Illinois Board of Higher Education to convert to LCS. McGregor stated that the amount given would probably cover keypunching some few data elements, for example, call number and author. It probably would not cover such subtle in-house costs as editing, proofreading or corrections. In fact, McGregor noted that 21 cents per record might not even cover all direct conversion costs if OCLC were used.

In converting through use of OCLC, a library must pay for the retrospective conversion charge per record, part-time help and terminal leasing or purchase. Originally retrospective conversion directly through OCLC was free, then it went to 5 cents per title. Effective July 1, 1982, the per record charge for non-prime time was 22 cents for new conversion projects, which is considerably less than the 65 cents prime time cost. That charge is scheduled to be in effect for 18 months, after which it is expected to increase. It should be noted that the charges quoted above apply only to projects that have been given special OCLC authorization for retrospective conversion.

If a library wants to combine conversion with catalog card production, it must pay the regular OCLC charges for cataloging. As of late 1982, the OCLC first-time usage (FTU) charge for cataloging was $1.46 per title cataloged, plus a fee for each card ordered. For 1983-1984, it is expected that the FTU will rise to approximately $1.55.

As Butler, Aveney and Scholz noted in their 1978 discussion of conversion, it is impossible to give detailed costs for a particular library conversion in a general work.[32] In general, the current range is from 22 cents per record, plus network fees (approximately 5% to 20%), to as much as $6.00 per record if contracted with a vendor. The average cost, of course, would be somewhere in between, with $2.00 per record being common.

Specific costs cannot be estimated here because there are many different tasks in each bibliographic conversion project and many different methods possible to accomplish them. In addition, the standards adhered to will influence the ultimate cost, as will the elements of the conversion process that are included in the calculation of a cost per record. For example, fixed costs may or may not be included; that is, a library may choose to include in actual costs only those items not being paid for already. For example, it might include costs of per-record retrospective conversion at non-prime time with OCLC, but not include a proportionate amount of salary for a full-time staff member who may serve as immediate supervisor of the data conversion project.

A library must also consider "hidden" costs, particularly when estimating in-house versus vendor-supplied conversion. A vendor's per-record charge may be moderate (for instance, $1.00 per record for 400,000 records), but the total cost may turn out to be prohibitive when all the factors are carefully analyzed. Some libraries have elected to use a vendor and have then changed their minds.

For example, Rice University Library originally determined that conversion via a vendor would be more cost-effective than doing an in-house project. (It calculated its in-house cost at $1.35 per title for 425,000 titles, or a total of $573,750.) However, using the vendor would have meant completing, and paying for, the project in less than two years. Therefore, the Rice University administration mandated that the conversion take place in-house in order to spread the costs out over a longer period of time.[33] At that time, the library recalculated costs and developed an estimate of $326,000-$466,000, spread over up to four years.

It must be remembered that vendors must recover their costs and also make a profit. Significantly higher costs with a vendor are probably routine. The higher costs need to be evaluated against the hidden costs of an in-house effort: the need for training of staff, supervision, terminal time and other resource-related requirements. Further discussion of comparative costs appears in Chapter 5.

Obtaining Funds

Whether a library chooses to find adequate funds in segments or tries to guarantee all necessary monies at the outset, actually securing the funds is a critical, essential and often difficult part of the conversion effort. Libraries must automate, which requires data conversion, in order to advance. However, to automate requires capital investment in the newer technologies, more and higher standards, and increased capabilities.

How does a library secure the necessary funding to pay for data conversion? The main funding sources are: the local institution, city, state and national government, and private foundations. A single library may seek support from all three sources in order to gather sufficient funds to undertake a data conversion, particularly a retrospective conversion effort.

Much of the funding for retrospective conversion projects in the late 1970s and early 1980s came from one of two government sources. Almost all states used some or all of their funds from the Library Services and Construction Act (LSCA) to fund retrospective conversion projects. The goal was to get the bibliographic information for most of the library resources in the state into machine-readable form in order to facilitate resource sharing and interlibrary loans within the state. Examples of states that used LSCA funds

for a major effort of this kind are Illinois, Pennsylvania, New York and South Dakota. Many public libraries and some academic and other libraries received support for retrospective conversion efforts from LSCA funding.

The other primary source of government funding for retrospective conversion was the Higher Education Act (HEA) Title II-C program. Most of this funding went to large research libraries, the majority of which were academic libraries, although some special and large public libraries were among the recipients. Libraries benefiting from Title II-C have input data into RLIN or OCLC, and both of those data bases have been greatly enriched through this process. The records converted have included monographic titles, serial titles, titles in microform and manuscripts. These large projects have helped to decrease the amount of original input required in most conversion projects using either OCLC or RLIN. However, it is not unrealistic to expect that a large research library with an old collection that includes many foreign-language materials should have in the range of 15% of its shelflist that is not in the data base of a bibliographic utility.

We would like to encourage library managers to consider conversion even if it is not readily apparent how they can provide the necessary financial resources. There are many creative ways to cover the costs of retrospective conversion. With the exception of fixed costs, which must be paid to a bibliographic utility or other source data base, not all costs need to result in actual outlay of dollars. Suggestions in this area include the use of volunteer labor and barter of equipment use or services. Other methods for accomplishing data conversion can minimize cash outlay.

Some libraries have received part or all of their funding for retrospective conversion from private granting agencies, such as foundations. Libraries with access to local foundations should not overlook them as a source of support for retrospective conversion projects. As we have stated, each situation is different, and each planning effort must take into account local factors or circumstances. When there is a determination to undertake a conversion effort, in most cases, with a little creative thinking, it will be possible to find the necessary resources to meet associated costs. (See the bibliography for citations to books and periodicals that provide suggestions on obtaining funding for projects such as retrospective conversion.)

Local Environment

The local environment is an intangible factor that may be either a plus or minus in planning for data conversion. Despite the fact that it is not quantifiable, it can be important in conversion planning and, ultimately, in the success of either one-time or ongoing conversion efforts. *Local* can refer to the institution as a whole, the entire library or the parts of the library where the work will take place. The environment can be influenced for the better by a positive leader who can articulate goals and objectives and develop a team spirit among those involved. Alternatively, if high-level key personnel resist conversion, their negative approach can drag down a whole effort.

From the standpoint of the people involved, the more input they have in the planning process, the greater will be their commitment to making it work and the greater will be their acceptance of the new machine-readable files. This applies not just to data conversion but to all library automation, and to change in general. Some institutions have made a point of including faculty members or other patrons in the planning process from the beginning. Users of the data can be particularly helpful in determining the scope and limits of a restrospective conversion. For example, should it be limited by date of publication and/or subject, or should it be comprehensive?

In general, positive leadership and a willingness to change and to attempt major projects are important elements in successful data conversion. They imply flexibility as difficulties are encountered or various options open up. They also imply a willingness to acknowledge when something simply will not work and consequently to accept a revision of established plans. How well people work together is often influenced by the style and leadership qualities of management. There is an increasing emphasis today in library education on management skills.[34] There is no question that library data conversion projects will benefit from the participation of individuals who have management and leadership skills.

EVALUATION AND DECISION MAKING

A library staff that accepts the concept of a data conversion project must still evaluate the data gathered in the planning process. As noted at the outset of this chapter, even a library staff that has decided to convert its files must still decide how it is going to accomplish the conversion. When a manager evaluates a library's situation, he or she must first decide whether the library is capable of supporting an in-house conversion project. This is the initial and most basic decision. Then, whether the decision is to go forward with the conversion in-house, to use a vendor or to combine methods, the library can proceed to the project design phase.

If the library manager is undecided about both the scope of the project and the best method of accomplishing it, it might be most appropriate to reach an agreement on scope first, and then to determine method.

Library managers may also analyze a conversion project starting with the issue of timing. Their approach would involve three questions:

1. Should a data conversion project be undertaken at this time?
2. If so, what should be the scope of the project?
3. What method should be selected to accomplish the conversion?

After these questions are answered, the library can begin project design. If the answer to the first question is no, the project must be put aside temporarily.

A careful review and evaluation of all the factors discussed in this chapter may lead to the conclusion that a data conversion project is not immediately appropriate for a given library. This decision, of course, does not preclude future options to undertake a data conversion effort. In many cases, circumstances (including technological advances) will alter to the point where a conversion project will become appropriate.

SUMMARY

From the time a library decides to establish or investigate a data conversion effort, either retrospective or prospective, or both, it should plan carefully. Planning should include establishment of the goals and objectives, description of the present situation, identification and analysis of alternatives, evaluation of available resources and deciding on formats and standards to be followed.

Data, once converted, have the potential to outlast any system in which they are first used. This is especially true if the conversion is done in accordance with national formats and standards. In general, the more complete the conversion of the data initially, the more options the library has to make use of the data in the future. Whether a library is converting data to support acquisitions, circulation or an online catalog, it will ultimately want to secure management information from its automated records as a system by-product. For any of these purposes, complete conversion will provide the capacity for later analyses.

If, because of some serious constraint of time or money or the need to demonstrate a product, the library settles for partial conversion of individual records, it should select the data elements to be included with consideration for future expansion. The library should be sure that those data elements initially converted are in accordance with national standards if it expects to readily expand the records or if it anticipates someday sharing records with a larger multi-institutional system or network.

Whenever the library decides to undertake the project, the next step after initial analysis is project design. That is the subject of the next chapter.

NOTES

1. Nancy John, "Preparing for Online Access: Retrospective Conversion," *Illinois Libraries* 62(7): 619 (September 1980).

2. Deanna Marcum and Richard Boss, "Information Technology," *Wilson Library Bulletin* 56(10): 765 (June 1982).

3. Barbara Radke and Teresa Montgomery, "CALLS ISSN Project," *Serials Review* 8(2): 67 (Summer 1982).

4. William Gray Potter, "Plans for an On-line Catalog at the University of Illinois," *Resource Sharing & Library Networks* 1(1): 53-63 (Fall 1981).

5. Ruth C. Carter, "Shelflist," *Encyclopedia of Library and Information Science* 27: 332-336 (1979).

6. Brett Butler, Brian Aveney and William Scholz, "The Conversion of Manual Catalogs to Collections Data Bases," *Library Technology Reports* 14(2): 201-203 (March-April 1978).

7. Ibid.

8. "Library Information Access System—LIAS—Library Automation for the 1980s and Beyond" (College Park, PA: Pennsylvania State University, n.d.).

9. Richard De Gennaro, "Libraries & Networks in Transition: Problems and Prospects for the 1980s," *Library Journal* 106: 1045-49 (May 15, 1981).

10. Linda F. Crismond, "Quality Issues in Retrospective Conversion Projects," *Library Resources & Technical Services* 25(1): 48-55 (January-March 1981).

11. Carolyn A. Johnson, "Retrospective Conversion of Three Library Collections," *Information Technology and Libraries* 1(2): 133 (June 1982).

12. Paul Metz, "Integrating Automation at Virginia Tech," *Wilson Library Bulletin* 56(4): 262 (December 1981).

13. *Anglo-American Cataloguing Rules,* 2d ed. (Chicago: American Library Association, 1978).

14. Michael S. Malinconico and Paul J. Fasana, *The Future of the Catalog: The Library's Choices* (White Plains, NY: Knowledge Industry Publications, 1979), pp. 21-22.

15. Ruth C. Carter, "Standards: One That's Missing," *LITA Newsletter,* p. 8 (Spring 1982).

16. Anton R. Pierce, "Draft Outline for the Need to Establish a MARC Format for Library Locations, Collections, and Inventory," (Blacksburg, VA: Virginia Polytechnic Institute and State University, 1981).

17. "News from the Field—MARC Format for Holdings," *RTSD Newsletter,* 7(4): 36 (July-August 1982).

18. *OCLC Newsletter,* no. 134, p. 4 (January 16, 1981).

19. Malinconico and Fasana, pp. 35-36.

20. Ibid., p. 38.

21. Douglas Ferguson, Neal K. Kaske, Gary S. Lawrence, Joseph R. Matthews and Robert Zich, "The CLR Public Online Catalog Study: An Overview," *Information Technology and Libraries* 1(2): 84-97 (June 1982).

22. James F. Govan, "The Union Catalogue: The Objectives and Economics in Perspective," in C. Donald Cook, ed., *The Future of the Union Catalogue: Proceedings,* Vol. 2 (New York: Haworth Press, 1982), p. 12.

23. Michael Gorman, "Fate, Time, Occasion, Chance, and Change; or How the Machine May Yet Save LCSH," *American Libraries* 11(9): 557-558 (October 1980).

24. Govan, p. 21.

25. Pierce, p. 1.

26. Elaine Rast, "Conversion Strategies for a Machine-Readable Data Base at Northern Illinois University Libraries," *Illinois Libraries* 62(7): 617 (September 1980).

27. Lou Wetherbee, "Planning a Retrospective Conversion Project," *ARL Spec Kit No. 65:* 5 (June 1980).

28. Pat Barkalow, "Conversion of Files for Circulation Control," *Journal of Library Automation* 12(3): 212-213 (September 1979).

29. Robert P. Holley and Dale Flecker, "Processing OCLC MARC Subscription Tapes at Yale University," *Journal of Library Automation* 12(1): 88 (March 1979).

30. William C. Horner, "Processing OCLC MARC Subscription Tapes at North Carolina State University," *Journal of Library Automation* 12(1): 91-94 (March 1979).

31. James Wilson McGregor, "LCS: Costs of Implementation and Use," *Illinois Libraries* 64(1): 51 (January 1982), p. 51.

32. Butler, Aveney and Scholz, p. 129.

33. Rice University librarians, verbal presentation on retrospective conversion planning. ALA RTSD/LITA Retrospective Conversion Discussion Group (San Francisco, June 28, 1981).

34. "A Conversation with Norman Horrocks," *Technicalities* 2(6): 10-12 (June 1982).

3

Planning for Data Conversion: Project Design

A data conversion effort, either retrospective or prospective, must be designed with extreme care. The more thorough the design of the project, the greater the chances will be for reaching the stated goals and objectives within the targeted time frame and budget. Major decisions that must be made once a library has committed itself to undertaking a conversion process will be examined in this chapter. At this point, detail will count. If a library can identify exactly all steps of the process and all the component elements, it will avoid unanticipated developments that could seriously interfere with the timely and efficient accomplishment of the data conversion.

DEVELOPMENT OF SPECIFICATIONS

No conversion effort can proceed effectively without specifications in advance. Specifications are equally important whether the project will be done in the library or outside by a vendor. In fact, before a vendor can quote a cost for data conversion, it must have the library's specifications. The vendor's price will depend on these, as well as on how much work must be done, the nature of the file(s) to be converted and established time frames.

What are specifications for conversion of manual records to machine-readable format? Briefly, specifications establish the criteria for the new machine record as contrasted with the existing manual record. They describe the source files to be converted, identify tasks to be performed, establish editing standards, and outline the necessary steps to accomplish all of the above. Specifications establish the quality of the machine-readable records that will be created as a result of the conversion. This does not mean that there is necessarily any right or best set of specifications that would apply to all libraries. For example, specifications for conversion of a bibliographic file may say that all machine records must exactly match all manual records. Or, the specifications can provide for accepting a fuller machine record from a vendor of a bibliographic utility's data base than may be present in the library's file. In that case, only call numbers and holdings information may need to be entered because they are specific to the local library.

Often the decision on how much of the record in a source data base can be accepted depends on how much authority control a library already has established. This is particularly important with regard to *AACR2* forms of headings and will be discussed in more detail in Chapter 4. For example, the specifications adopted by Rice University for matching its local catalog records against the records in the OCLC data base called for exactly matching its shelflist card to the machine-readable record.[1] However, because Rice already had established a good mechanism for authority control, the Rice librarians did decide to accept *AACR2* headings even though a pre-*AACR2* form of heading was in the local catalog record.

Individual File Specifications

Specifications must be developed for each separate file to be converted. A file that is mostly bibliographic may have quite different specifications from one that has other types of data elements, such as circulation, acquisition or dealer data. For some files the only conversion may be prospective. For others, particularly bibliographic files, the conversion may be retrospective. In either case, the specific data elements in each file should be identified and the conversion criteria for each data element clearly stated. Specifications for converting specific data elements can range from converting only the most recent payment records to changing the imprint field (260 tag in a MARC record) if it does not match the local record character for character. Specifications should indicate, for example, whether or not extra subject headings in the source file should be left in the machine-readable record if they are not in the library's catalog record. They should indicate whether or not to fill in fixed fields if the records did not originally include fixed fields.

One way of developing specifications for the conversion of bibliographic records is to specify the fields that must be compared in order for the record found in the source data base to match that in the library's catalog. Krieger, writing on the retrospective conversion at the library of Miami University-Hamilton, OH, said that Miami-Hamilton's specifications were to check the following fields:[2]

010	LCCN	If present
1xx	Main Entry	All subfields
245	Title	Up to subfield *b*
250	Edition	If present
260	Imprint	All subfields
300	Collation	Arabic pagination only

More fields were checked in the retrospective conversion of the shelflist of the Thomas Cooper Library (the main library) of the University of South Carolina. The Cooper Library specifications called for checking the following fields when a work represented by one of its shelflist records was found in the OCLC data base: 010, 090/092, 1xx, 245, 250, 260, 300, 4xx, 5xx, 6xx, 7xx, and 8xx.[3]

In summary, some libraries want all fields edited to match local records, other libraries care only about selected fields and still others will take all data in the source data base with adjustments for nothing except purely local information, such as call numbers. Obviously, a large range of options exists in conversion of bibliographic data. Each individual library staff must draft specifications with consideration for its overall goals and objectives.

Treatment of Data Elements

In developing conversion specifications for bibliographic records that are found in a local shelflist and matched against an online data base with MARC and contributed records, a number of decisions must be made in regard to each data element of each record:

1. Should the online record always be preferred for all fields (except local information such as call number)?

2. Should the online record be preferred for some fields and the local record for others?

3. Should the local library's data always be preferred?

4. Does preference for data in the online record depend in whole or in part on its cataloging source; for example, does Library of Congress cataloging carry more weight than the cataloging of the library doing the conversion, or contributed or member copy?

Each library planning a conversion project must answer those questions. When different data elements receive different treatment, the specifications need to carefully delineate the treatment required for each separate element.

Long-term Implications

In drawing up specifications for a retrospective conversion it is wise to remember the long-term implications. As many writers have stressed, the machine-readable data base is a long-term investment that is likely to outlast any system for which it was first used (see, for example, Metz, quoting Tamar Uluaker).[4] To the extent that funds, staff and other resources permit, the specifications should call for the conversion of full records in accordance with nationally accepted standards. Even if partial records are accepted, those data elements present should be in accordance with standards. If they are bibliographic records, they should be MARC compatible. In general, it will be easier and more cost-effective to do data conversion in accordance with accepted standards the first time around than to try to upgrade records later.

PROCEDURES FOR THE CONVERSION PROCESS

Just as it is essential to develop specifications for the actual data to be converted, it is essential to firmly establish procedures to be followed in the conversion process. They should be simple, clear, efficient in design of work flow and use of staff time, and thorough. They should be in writing and they should provide for control and monitoring of the progress made.

The written procedures will need to indicate how many drawers can be removed from the shelflist at one time, how problem records are to be flagged and how records which have been converted should be identified. They should also indicate how to mark records that need original input and how to record statistics on work accomplished. They should provide instructions for filing into completed portions of files. The foregoing list is not complete, but is indicative of the kinds of procedures that must be considered.

One of the first decisions to be made with regard to bibliographic files is whether the library will bar code and/or inventory its collection and shelflist, and if so, when.

In most cases bar coding and inventory are treated as one package. Data conversion to support circulation requires that it be addressed as part of conversion planning. If an online catalog is the first objective, decisions on bar coding and inventory may not be made prior to the conversion, but they must be considered. Bar coding, once initiated, becomes a part of prospective conversion and must be included in the planning for current work flow. Whether a retrospective data conversion project is to be performed by a vendor or in-house, there are three basic options on the proper timing for bar coding. They are:

1. Bar code the books before the conversion. (This implies an inventory prior to conversion.)

2. Bar code the shelflist at the time of conversion and the books afterward. (This is a de facto inventory after the conversion and means that the newly converted data base must be brought into line with actual holdings.)

3. Bar code both the shelflist and the books after conversion. (This, too, represents an inventory after conversion. It also requires that all records, or at least records for items that circulate, be called up for a second time.) If there is no inventory after conversion, the data base will probably contain many items that the library no longer holds. The alternative to an inventory is to bar code items as they circulate for retrospective materials and as they are acquired for new additions to a library's collection.

A library data conversion to support circulation and/or inventory must go beyond the conversion of bibliographic records that pertain to each title. It must identify and provide a means of retrieving each separate physical piece represented by a single bibliographic record. As De Klerk points out, bar coding provides the mechanism for labeling and identifying each item in a collection.[5] (Issues related to bar coding will be discussed further under "individual item controls," later in this chapter, and in Chapter 4.)

PROJECT STAFF

If the conversion is to be done in the library, the project design must provide for the number and type of people needed. Determination of necessary staff depends on the type and quantity of tasks to be accomplished, and the equipment, space and/or financial resources available. These in turn depend on the length of time allotted to the project. If retrospective conversion is done in the library, additional staff may be needed for that specific purpose. Job descriptions will need to be developed and recruitment initiated. Different levels of staff will be involved because conversion requires a variety of tasks of varying degrees of difficulty, from simply copying data to original cataloging. In all cases, the project must have a supervisor. This may be someone hired specifically for that purpose or it may be a member of the library's regular staff.

If the in-house retrospective conversion project involves bibliographic data, the project supervisor should be a librarian. The project supervisor will monitor progress, schedule staff and resolve problems, including those requiring a professional knowledge of cataloging rules. Depending upon the specifications for conversion and the complexity of bibliographic data to be converted, project staff may also be librarians. However, in the majority of cases, well-trained student assistants or staff personnel will be able to handle the conversion of most bibliographic records. Normally there will be several project members working under each supervisor.

When a data conversion project involves other types of library records, such as subscription payments, accounting records or other nonbibliographic records, it is less important that the immediate supervisor be a librarian. It is more likely that the project supervisor will be a member of the library's regular staff who has considerable familiarity with the files that are being converted. As with all factors involved in data conversion, there are no hard and fast rules. Actual staffing decisions for an in-house effort depend on the nature of the particular project, the availability of regular or temporary personnel, financial resources, and other immediate circumstances.

If retrospective conversion is contracted for outside the library, some work still must be done by the library's staff. Personnel will be responsible for monitoring progress, keeping statistical records, and, most important in terms of time, resolving problems. The last normally includes original input of records not found in the source data base.

Prospective conversion ordinarily will be done by library staff. It is likely that job descriptions will need to be rewritten and staff given additional training. In some cases, job classifications may need to be upgraded if data entry is complex. In ongoing conversion, entry of data into machine-readable format takes the place of manual recording and manipulation of data. Although parallel systems may be maintained for a short period, a machine-based system is expected to supersede a manual system. Therefore, it is appropriate to restructure the jobs of the staff involved.

Often staff hired for data conversion, especially major retrospective projects, are expected to work evenings and/or weekends. Advertising and interviews for temporary conversion project staff must state clearly the duties of the job (which may range from data entry to problem solving), the hours of work, the salary and the necessary qualifications. They should describe all conditions of hire (will the work be temporary or permanent, part-time or full-time). It should be noted again that contracting with a vendor is often more expensive because the vendor is recovering costs and also making a profit. However, the vendor has the administrative responsibility for hiring staff, keeping appropriate payment and personnel records and the like. As in most aspects of a data conversion job, no approach is equally good for all libraries. Decisions made with regard to project staff will vary with each situation.

TIMETABLE FOR THE PROJECT

Project design should always include the establishment of a realistic timetable. Planners, whether systems analysts or other personnel, are often instructed to determine what is a reasonable schedule, if there are no complications, and then multiply it by a suitable factor, such as two. This is wise in any project and particularly so in a data conversion project, which is both labor intensive and dependent on machine performance. Reliability and response time can be significant factors in a conversion that uses source records from a bibliographic utility. Down time and/or poor response time on a system such as OCLC or Research Libraries Information Network (RLIN) can significantly slow a project. In addition, part-time or temporary staff may have a high turnover rate, and there will always be such factors as vacations and illnesses.

The timetable should be developed for the whole project, with more detail for the early stages, such as the first phase or the first quarter or perhaps the first year. It is recommended that target goals be established for various key points along the way. Establishing goals for conversion completion at several stages will help to monitor progress and assure that the project stays on or close to schedule. This is important because the schedule will usually be based on the funding and the number of people to be employed with the funds.

Obviously, before a schedule can be developed, it is necessary to know how long it would ordinarily take to convert a given number of records. Butler, Aveney and Scholz list the following factors that influence costs:

1. Size and percent of the collection being converted;

2. Publication dates of the items being converted;

3. Languages represented in the records being converted;

4. Relative fullness of the converted records;

5. Percentage of titles in the collection not in the source data base;

6. How closely the cataloging in the library's collection matches current national standards;

7. Number of staff members available to work on conversion.[6]

In order to get a feeling for the time involved, the library manager will need to test a representative sample. Once an average time per record is developed, the number of staff members needed for a particular period of time can be determined. Then the library may choose to do all the easy files or records first and save the difficult ones for later.

The conversion rate of bibliographic records may be as low as three per man-hour, if such conversion elements such as stack checking, bar coding and problem solving are figured into overall production time. On the other hand, if the figure calculated represents only updates possible at a data entry point, with no allowance for offline activities such as those mentioned above, a figure of 40-50 or more records per man-hour may be derived when the conversion is done through a utility such as OCLC or RLIN. It should be noted that a conversion figure of 40 or more is for shelflist records with the Library of Congress (LC) card number present and editing done for no more than two or three variable fields. When the conversion is done through another agency, such as the Carrollton Press, Inc. Retrospective MARC (REMARC) data base, a clerk may be able to enter keys for 100 or more records per hour.[7] (That figure does not include checking records for errors or multiple hits or solving other problems.)

INDIVIDUAL ITEM CONTROLS

A conversion project may be limited to bibliographic data, with plans to enter item-specific data at another time. However, many conversion projects, both retrospective and ongoing, deal with data for specific physical items. Conversion to a system for the purpose of supporting inventory, circulation or acquisitions and in-process tracking including serials check-in will require some means of identifying each separate physical item. The design of the project plan will require decisions in at least three areas related to each separate physical item:

1. Should each item get a machine-readable label such as a bar code or optical character recognition (OCR) label, or a label that combines the two?

2. Should there be a physical inventory as part of the conversion process?

3. What standards and formats should be used to communicate holdings or physical-piece information?

The third decision—on standards and formats—might be considered part of specifications development. It is listed here, however, because the library file being converted may not carry data on each item in a standard format. In that case the design of the project may need to provide for time to reformat holdings statements. It is often necessary to consult the individual pieces in order to identify and describe them correctly.

Bar Coding

If a library manager decides to put bar code and/or OCR labels on the materials, each label by necessity pertains to a physical piece. The exception to this would be in special formats such as microfiche or media kits, where one bar code could conceivably cover multiple physical pieces contained in one cover. In these cases, the items would normally circulate in the covering envelope or other container.

As previously noted, if a library decides to bar code its collection, it must decide at which point in the conversion process this is to be done. Once bar coding has been introduced it becomes part of prospective conversion and that also must be planned for. In ongoing conversion efforts, bar coding may take place at different points depending on the system it helps support. An integrated system that starts with the acquisitions process will usually provide for bar coding of each new item at the time it is received. A system limited to circulation could conceivably bar code items at the time of first circulation or at the time of cataloging.

There is no perfect plan that will fit all situations; each library must try to determine what will be most efficient and cost-effective in terms of its own circumstances. In general, one should attempt to have each physical piece handled and each machine-readable record accessed as few times as possible in order to maximize use of staff time and generally reduce costs.

Advantages and Disadvantages of an Inventory

The decision on whether or not to inventory the collection as part of the conversion process may be a factor in the decision concerning bar coding. It can also be an independent consideration. Should a librarian elect not to have an inventory as part of the conversion, he or she should understand very clearly the implications of that decision. Some advantages of performing an inventory are:

1. Resources will not be wasted converting items no longer in the collection.

2. Users of the machine-readable data base will not be frustrated by searching for materials no longer in the library.

3. An inventory will determine which items need rebinding or repair, so that bar coding can be postponed until after the repairs.

4. An inventory provides an opportunity to weed items from the collection.

5. An inventory allows all components of the record of any item to be accessed or handled only once.

Inventory of the collection as part of a conversion also has disadvantages:

1. It shifts more costs up front, because people and time are needed to do the inventory.

2. It holds up the actual conversion process by the amount of time taken to do the inventory.

CAPTURE OF THE CONVERTED RECORDS

"Capture of the records" after the conversion refers to how the records converted to machine-readable form will be made available to the library for its use. The variety of options a library has in this regard will depend in part on whether it does its conversion in-house or through a vendor.

Three primary methods are available for converting to machine-readable form for use by the individual library. They are: through offline products, through a "black box" interface or through direct input to a local system. Each of these is discussed below.

Offline Products or Batch Processing

This method most commonly uses magnetic tape either from a vendor who does the conversion or from a bibliographic utility used as the source data base for the data conversion. One must know exactly what format the data will be in, which code and density the data will be stored in, and also the frequency with which the library will receive tapes. Once the system is operational, the library may require tapes more frequently than it did during conversion.

"Archive" tapes from OCLC are the most widespread of the tape products. They are received through subscription either directly by the library or through the network of which the library is a member. In the latter case, the network can provide the library with a copy of its own records, which have been "stripped" off the network archive tape. In dealing with tape products it is important to note that they must be stored under carefully controlled conditions of temperature and humidity and recopied approximately every 12 months.

Machine-readable records can also be captured by the library in other offline products. These include hard or floppy discs, cassettes, etc. However, tapes are easiest to handle, store and ship, and are most frequently encountered.

In some cases libraries do retrospective and/or prospective data conversion with no immediate plans to get the data in machine-readable form for use in the library. Instead, the library may receive an offline product. For example, a library may undertake data conversion with the goal of receiving a computer output microform (COM) catalog as its only product. That COM catalog may be either microfiche or microfilm. Of course, a library that does its own conversion into a bibliographic utility may receive a tape first and then get a COM catalog. However, a library that contracts for its conversion with a vendor may never receive the tape product or any other material in which the records are in machine-readable form. Some libraries that have done conversion for the purpose of a COM catalog are the University of Texas at Dallas, Western Kentucky University and the Chicago Public Library.[8,9,10]

The "Black Box" Interface

The "black box" interface caused quite a stir when it was first announced in 1979.[11] The original was developed at Sacramento State College by three Californians: Jerry Kline, Steve Silverstein and Lochman Sippy. It was connected to the OCLC terminal on one side and, via the OCLC printer port, to the CL Systems, Inc. (CLSI) LIBS 100 circulation system on the other side. What was so exciting about the black box was that it made possible the transfer of converted machine-readable records from OCLC directly into an individual library's system, whether a vendor turnkey system such as the CLSI LIBS 100 or a system developed in-house. The machine-to-machine connection eliminated the need for tapes, which had the built-in drawback of a time lag, and required storage and maintenance, as well.

Since the original black box became available, it has been replicated many times. Most turnkey automated system vendors now have the capability of a machine-to-machine connection or are developing it. Microcomputers can be programmed readily to perform this function. For libraries with some local expertise or with the means to back up a local machine system, it is now possible to save steps and time by eliminating the need for tape-loading data. (See Chapter 7.) Nevertheless, tapes are still the most common manner of receiving machine-readable records and can be expected to hold that position for much of the 1980s.

There seems little doubt, however, that there will be more direct connections between bibliographic utilities and systems in individual libraries, whether those systems are locally or commercially developed and supported. In addition, machine-to-machine connections can be expected to grow in the other direction—from a library to a utility. A prototype in this area will be the machine-to-machine interface developed by the Pennsylvania State University Library to communicate its bibliographic records to RLIN.[12]

Input Directly to a Local System

A great deal of data conversion is done by individual libraries on-site into a computer confined to the library or its parent institution. This is true for all sizes and types of libraries and for all library functions. A high percentage of data conversion to support circulation and acquisitions (including serials control) is handled locally. Although cataloging is usually done through a bibliographic utility, existing machine-readable catalog records most commonly are maintained locally. If maintenance is conducted through a repeat of the input process to a bibliographic utility, there will be a wait for tapes (unless there is a machine-to-machine interface which does not require tapes). To avoid this delay, virtually all online systems provide a means for local data entry of both entire records and updates. In general, it is much easier and more efficient to maintain item-specific information in-house.

Some large university libraries have developed or are developing local systems through which they do all of their data conversion for all types of records. Two of the most notable examples are Northwestern University and the Pennsylvania State University. Both libraries have purchased a subscription to the MARC tapes and otherwise have input directly into their own systems rather than going through a bibliographic utility in order to capture their catalog records in machine-readable form.

Northwestern University

Northwestern On-Line Total Integrated System (NOTIS) at the Northwestern University Library, is well-described in the literature. Articles by Aagard and Veneziano appeared as early as 1972.[13,14] NOTIS was built on the principle that data converted to machine-readable format once can serve multiple purposes.[15] Its single data base supports acquisitions, serials control, cataloging and the online catalog, and connects with the online circulation system, as well.

Because Northwestern's system is used for acquisitions, its conversion of bibliographic as well as order information begins at that point. When an item is to be ordered, and if there is no record for the title already in the NOTIS data base, the searcher creates a provisional bibliographic record and also a copy holdings record. If appropriate, the MARC data base is also searched and if the search is successful, the MARC data transfer to the provisional NOTIS record. Records not upgraded from MARC will have the provisional bibliographic data supplemented by the data necessary to place an order. Information for titles on order displays in the public catalog, and all staff with terminals have immediate access to order and receipt data.

Northwestern's system shows the power of an integrated system where most data conversion is essentially done locally.

Pennsylvania State University

The Pennsylvania State University library system plans a total retrospective conversion of its catalog and is committed to prospective conversion. Penn State closed its card catalog January 1, 1981 and has records created since that time available in a COM fiche catalog.[16] An online catalog supporting the needs of both library staff and patrons will be available probably by 1984. As noted above, Penn State has purchased the MARC tapes. It retains the current three years' records online and will use them as the source for records for its bibliographic data base whenever possible. Many of the shelflist records which Penn State has converted have been keyed into its local system in their entirety by Penn State staff, even though they may have previously been put into machine-readable form when Penn State was an online cataloging participant with OCLC (through 1980).

Data input into Penn State's system is very rapid for several reasons. One reason response time is always good is that the library owns the computer and is not competing for its use. Another factor is that Penn State has exhaustive procedural manuals for inputting and also believes in intensive training and careful review of new input staff. In this way it achieves a high degree of accuracy with little need for correction.

A third factor is that when Penn State converts its data into its local system, conversion is to the standards that existed at the time the record was first cataloged. Consequently, the data conversion is not slowed for upgrading to *AACR2*, for example. This does not mean that Penn State is ignoring the problem of authority control and current standards. On the contrary, because Penn State has always done exhaustive authority work and plans to put its authority file in machine-readable form as an integral part of its system, it does not need to change headings at the time of data conversion. Penn State expects to make the authority system transparent to the user. The result of a search will not depend on the form of heading used as an access point because the system will make the link internally. This syndetic structure is called "Universal Entry Control" and is part of the Remote Catalog Access module under development for Penn State's Library Information Access System (LIAS).[17]

Choosing the Best Method

Three basic methods of capturing the converted data have been described. Each method can be effective if properly applied in an appropriate situation. Because many libraries begin conversion in advance of an operational local computer system, the method most frequently employed will be the receipt of converted data by offline products, especially tapes. Both the second and third methods (direct interface between source data base and local system, and input directly into local system) are possible only when there is a local system operational.

Even if there is a local system operational, most libraries will choose to convert their bibliographic records by going through one of the bibliographic utilities such as Washington Library Network (WLN), RLIN or OCLC. By so doing, the library can take advantage of machine-readable records for items in its collection. At the same time, the library can participate in building a national data base that will include its resources along with those of other participants.

In general, only the very largest, or possibly the very smallest, highly specialized libraries can do direct data conversion in a cost-effective manner. Although a library can handle data conversion locally in a simplistic fashion with brief records, this would greatly limit its future options. It seems safe to say that local data conversion is ideal for maintaining existing bibliographic records and for nonbibliographic or holdings data. Use of an existing source data base for conversion of a library's shelflist is almost essential.

IMPLEMENTATION PHASE

The smoothness and the timely completion of a data conversion project will correlate directly with its advance planning. This is not to say that a few projects have not been successful with procedures developed as the need arose. However, in general, the implementation phase of a project succeeds in direct relationship to the extent and quality of the planning that preceded it. Careful planning, nonetheless, cannot prevent all problems. In fact if there is any rule in dealing with computers or related activities (which include data conversion), it is: "Expect the unexpected."

In order to make the actual project proceed as efficiently as possible, procedures should be formalized and written down. A general understanding among staff present at the onset of a project is not sufficient, since there will always be staff turnover. Another important rule in dealing with computers is: "Document, document!" If the data entered into machine-readable form are later to be decoded and applied, one must be able to determine exactly how they were entered. If practices in applying data in any particular field or fields vary over a period of time, this must be documented precisely. Furthermore, as McKinley pointed out, thorough documentation can "contribute to higher production levels and better quality work."[18] She added that project supervisors should have better than average writing skills.

Along with documentation of all procedures, interpretations and guidelines, there must be an effective work flow plan. As far as possible this must be determined in advance. However, this is by nature an iterative process. Personnel must expect that early experiences may lead to improvements in the work flow appropriate to any particular situation. During the implementation phase, personnel will be hired and trained, new equipment will be installed and tested, and various quality control procedures and management record-keeping will be initiated.

In the initial stages of implementation, a library should be prepared to resolve procedural "bugs." It may also find that a part of the specifications may be unworkable. Or, something unexpected may arise. In fact, if there is not at least one unanticipated snag it will be a very unusual conversion project! It is safe to say that overall progress will probably be slower than expected. On the other hand, if a realistic timetable was established and the project is inspired by a leader who can establish team goals, then the project has a good chance of meeting objectives and being on schedule.

When the conversion is contracted to a vendor, the library must still maintain control. Thus, implementation of the project will include monitoring progress, including a review of project statistics, and looking over the outputs of the project guaranteeing that established quality standards have been met. In addition, conversion contracted to a vendor requires that the library submit data in the quantities and at the time intervals specified. Also, one must provide for processing data to be added to the shelflist sections the vendor will have completed. Also, machine-readable data must be tested to determine their actual applicability to the local system, when one is already available. The initial part of implementation involves refining procedures, completing documentation, monitoring progress, keeping statistics and, most of all, assuring that in practice the data asked for and received are indeed what one needs.

SUMMARY

There are many details involved in designing a data conversion project, even if much of the project will be contracted out to a vendor. All projects require specifications for the conversion, documentation of formats and standards, and procedures to be followed. The last encompasses deciding who does what and when, and developing techniques for controlling quality and monitoring progress. The more carefully the project is thought out and documented at the design phase, the less chance there will be of major unforeseen complications or inadequacies later. Thorough planning will provide for revision of routines in an implementation phase. It will also take into account certain special considerations in the conversion effort. These considerations—conversion of serial records, reclassification, treatment of pre-*AACR2* records and individual item controls—are discussed in detail in Chapter 4.

Because data conversion has major long-term implications for benefits to the library, a careful planning process is well worth the investment of time and money. The library that plans carefully and thoroughly will be rewarded by a smooth conversion effort, which will indeed fulfill its goals and objectives in a timely, cost-effective manner. The advice to libraries should be: If you are not willing to adequately plan for a data conversion project, don't attempt one!

NOTES

1. "Retrospective Conversion Planning," Rice University librarians' verbal presentation, ALA RTSD/LITA Retrospective Conversion Discussion Group (San Francisco, CA, June 28, 1981).

2. Michael T. Krieger, "Retrospective Conversion at a Two-Year College," *Information Technology and Libraries* 1(1): 43 (March 1982).

3. Carolyn A. Johnson, "Retrospective Conversion of Three Library Collections," *Information Technology and Libraries* 1(2): 135 (June 1982).

4. Paul Metz, "Integrating Automation at Virginia Tech," *Wilson Library Bulletin* 56(4): 265 (December 1981).

5. Ann de Klerk, "Barcoding a Collection—Why, When and How," *Library Resources & Technical Services* 25(1): 82 (January/March 1981).

6. Brett Butler, Brian Aveney and William Scholz, "The Conversion of Manual Catalogs to Collections Data Bases," *Library Technology Reports* 14(2): 130 (March-April 1978).

7. "Vendor Profile," interview with William Buchanan, *Technicalities* 2(12): 5 (December 1982).

8. Richard W. Meyer and John F. Knapp, "COM Catalog Based on OCLC Records," *Journal of Library Automation* 8(4): 312-321 (December 1975).

9. Earl E. Wassom and Richard A. Jones, "Bibliographic Access to Full Descriptive Cataloging with COM," *Journal of Library Automation* 11(1): 47-53 (March 1978).

10. Donald Schabel, "Experience with a Computer Produced Catalog," *Illinois Libraries* 62(7): 609-613 (September 1980).

11. "Technology Notes: OCLC/CLSI Interface Announced," *LJ/SLJ Hotline* 8(8): 5 (February 26,1979).

12. Research Libraries Group, Inc. press release, "RLG/Local System Link Announced," [January 1982].

13. James S. Aagard, "An Interactive Computer-Based Circulation System: Design and Development," *Journal of Library Automation* 5(1): 3-11 (March 1972).

14. Velma Veneziano, "An Interactive Computer-Based Circulation System for Northwestern University: The Library Puts It to Work," *Journal of Library Automation* 13(4): 223 (December 1980).

15. Elizabeth Furlong, "A Case Study in Automated Acquisitions: Northwestern University Library," *Journal of Library Automation* 5(2): 101 (June 1972).

16. "Library Information Access System—LIAS—Library Automation for the 1980s and Beyond" (College Park, PA: Pennsylvania State University, n.d.).

17. "Library Automation at the Pennsyvlania State University: 'The LIAS System' " (Pennsylvania State University, October 1981).

18. Margaret McKinley, "A Pragmatic Approach to Serials Data Conversion," *Serials Review* 7(1): 90 (January/March 1981).

4

Special Considerations

A number of special considerations may be factors in a data conversion effort, whether that effort is retrospective, ongoing or both. The special considerations involved will vary from library to library. They will depend upon the nature of a library's collection, the reasons for undertaking the conversion, the files being converted and other circumstances. Four areas of consideration that are commonly encountered in data conversion efforts will be reviewed here. They are:

1. Conversion of serial records
2. Reclassification in conjunction with conversion
3. Treatment of pre-*AACR2* records
4. Bar coding or other individual item controls

CONVERSION OF SERIAL RECORDS

Gorman commented in 1975: "What is a serial? A serial is the biggest problem in librarianship."[1] The 1981 introduction of the *Anglo-American Cataloguing Rules, Second Edition* (*AACR2*) has served to exacerbate the problems of dealing with serials. Gorman cited serials' changes as being the major problem.[2] Carter supported the idea that serials have always presented problems and that the advent of *AACR2* only added one more level of complexity to an already complicated format of materials.[3]

The conversion of serial records—whether bibliographic records; order, receipt, renewal and payment records; or inventory and circulation records—requires special considerations and decisions. Serials are complicated for many reasons. For example, they change title and frequency of publication, they merge or split, they may be issued out of sequence, they suspend or cease publication and they start new numbering systems. In addition, the adoption of *AACR2* significantly changed the rules for entering serials titles in a bibliographic record.

Librarians undertaking conversion projects should not bypass serials because of their complications. It is the very complexity of serials that mitigates in favor of making them part of an initial conversion and an original and integral part of any automated data base. A data conversion plan or automated system that can handle serial records should readily encompass records of other materials, especially monographs. The reverse is not necessarily true.

The following discussion will consider conversion of serial bibliographic records in the context of the major "national" bibliographic conversion effort: CONversion of SERial Records (CONSER). Topics include inputting directly into a local data base, conversion of only the bibliographic records or both bibliographic and holdings records, and the relationship of a library's conversion to local, state, regional and/or national cooperative projects. The discussion will touch on union listing, including the OCLC union listing capability, as well as other serial finding tools. It will also consider aspects of serials cataloging that will normally need consideration in conversion. In addition, the conversion of data to support acquisition of serial materials and their control once in the library will be covered. It is hoped that this discussion will help librarians deal with the problems of serial records conversion in a way that will benefit the library and its users.

CONSER

The conversion of serial bibliographic records requires an understanding of the basics of CONSER. CONSER was initiated in 1973 when an ad hoc discussion group on serials data bases met at the American Library Association annual conference in Las Vegas.[4] CONSER's goal was to eliminate duplication of conversion for the same serial bibliographic records. It was thought that replication of conversion efforts could be avoided or minimized by cooperatively converting into a system that was widely available online and whose records also would be distributed on tape.

The goals of this project were widely supported. Before long, substantial support for the project, both financial and managerial, was provided by the Council on Library Resources.[5] The 12 initial participants anticipated that 200,000 to 300,000 serials titles would be converted into a machine-readable data base in two to three years.[6]

CONSER set up the standards to be followed for conversion of the bibliographic data. Some early decisions have left an impact on data conversion today in all but the most local conversions of serial bibliographic records. As Anable pointed out, machine-readable bibliographic files have three basic attributes: format, required depth of data elements and rules covering the construction of the data.[7] Anable described the background of bibliographic treatment of serials and gave five areas to be considered in comparing the various cataloging codes and standards that have existed over the years. His article preceded the introduction of *AACR2* but the principles discussed can be applied to that code also.

Because CONSER was well underway in the mid-1970s, it had many years to build a machine-readable data base before the implementation of *AACR2*. Those machine-readable records created in the CONSER effort are still widespread and a major factor in current decisions on the conversion of serial records.

LATEST TITLE VERSUS SUCCESSIVE TITLE CATALOGING

Of all the decisions made in the CONSER project, the most influential has been the one to allow both latest title and successive title cataloging. Latest title cataloging allows all changes for a single publication to be recorded in a single bibliographic entry. Successive title cataloging requires a separate record for each title change. Although CONSER's initial decision has since been modified, the policy has caused problems. Of course, it was a pragmatic decision because many of the participants did not feel that they could attempt a large-scale conversion effort and recatalog much of their serial collection at the same time. Had this variation from the current standards not been permitted, CONSER would have grown much less rapidly and, consequently, would have had much less impact.

Both the first (1967) and second editions of the *Anglo-American Cataloguing Rules* call for successive title cataloging. Many uses of converted serial bibliographic records either require or are best suited to successive entry treatment. Included in that category is the union listing component on OCLC, which functions most effectively with successive title records. Both the *American National Standards Institute (ANSI) Standard for Serial Holdings Statements at the Summary Level* and the draft of the *ANSI Standard for Serial Holdings Statements at the Detailed Level*[8,9] specify that holdings data should be associated with a bibliographic citation which, for all practical purposes, must be successive title cataloging.

A library must make a fundamental decision in regard to its handling of retrospective serials titles. Will it use a latest-entry record if that is the only available record already in machine-readable form? If not, will it recatalog the item to successive entry, or omit it initially from the converted file?

One should keep in mind that completely new cataloging for records new to the data base may be required if using some bibliographic utilities, including OCLC. New records must be in adherence with *AACR2*; this may include entry fields for titles that are already in the library's records in earlier forms. However, the CONSER libraries have proposed linking to existing records as they appear in the online CONSER data base. The question can then become: Should all earlier related titles be recataloged? Or, if not, how can all related records be linked for users?

Obviously, in dealing with serials titles, which are complicated because many related publications must be linked together, there are no easy answers. If maximum consistency and integrity are provided in related records and in the data base as a whole, cataloging production and/or conversion of serial bibliographic records may be unacceptably slow. A library must answer these conversion questions in light of its own schedule and resources and with cognizance of the rules for any outside data base (such as that of a bibliographic utility) that might be involved.

PURPOSES FOR CONVERSION OF SERIAL DATA

Before final decisions can be made on what data elements and detail from serial records should be converted, it is necessary to know how the converted data will be used. The purpose may be to support any of the following: acquisitions functions, including check-in, claiming and accounting; circulation/inventory control; catalog access whether online or computer output microform (COM); or an integrated comprehensive system.

A frequent purpose is better control or management of serial records. This has become increasingly true in recent years, as attempts at providing computer-assisted serials processing systems at reasonable cost, either locally or through a bibliographic utility, have been successful. As McKinley pointed out, a new wave of interest has been generated in the conversion of manual serial records to machine-readable form as a part of automated serials processing.[10] McKinley stresses the fact that before a library can obtain the benefits of automated processing systems, manual files must be put into machine-readable form. She makes the significant point that data conversion is not limited to transferring data from one format to another. It also requires skilled, intellectual effort in upgrading old, inconsistent and incomplete manual records.

Careful planning is most important in considering the conversion of serial records and files. Adequate time must be given to this phase and a conversion project should be undertaken only when the purpose or purposes behind it are clearly understood. In the case of serials control, a number of purposes are possible. They include:

1. To provide automated assists to the claiming process;

2. To provide widespread online access to the check-in files;

3. To provide automated assists in binding preparation and record keeping;

4. To make one data entry, such as a bibliographic citation or holding statement, serve many purposes so that data need not be rekeyed in multiple isolated systems.

In general, automation of serials check-in functions is seen as controlling and assisting time-consuming and labor-intensive functions such as preparation of binding tickets and claiming. Claiming, which involves identifying either specific issues which were missed or titles for which no issues have been received for months or years, is a tedious clerical function. Staff members are reluctant to scan manual files to determine which publications have not been received recently. The computer can readily assist that process.

Although conversion of records for serials control can provide access to check-in files, it will not save time in the check-in process itself. In most cases, check-in through an automated system requires approximately the same time as in a manual system.[11] More important, one entry of data into machine-readable form can be used for many purposes and up-to-the-minute receipt or other status data are widely available through an online system. This is true when the data are in machine-readable form through a bibliographic utility, such as was described in articles by Kamens and Buckeye.[12,13] It is also true if the data have been placed in machine-readable form in a system local to a single institution, such as those described by Willmering, and Harrison and Miller.[14,15]

Regardless of which purpose is most fundamental to a serials conversion effort, data must be tied to a bibliographic citation. Serials publications are often searched for by title. Historically, serials converted for finding tools such as union lists often had brief bibliographic citations—in many cases, limited to the title. As more serials data conversion is either online with a major bibliographic utility or an offshoot from one, there is an increased emphasis on having full bibliographic data available at least in a source file.

At the same time, the form and choice of entry may vary from local handling of the serial. However, all elements in the record need not match exactly, as long as the title proper is included in the library's data base. In other words, the "national" online CONSER record can be accepted as is, although it might vary from local records for the same publication. Again, this would depend on the organization and functions of locally maintained machine-readable records.

CONVERSION OF HOLDINGS DATA

Most functions related to serials publications will require some conversion of holdings data. Several issues are involved here. They include:

1. Should conversion of holdings be done at the same time and by the same method as conversion of bibliographic data?

2. What level of holdings will be converted, summary or detailed?

3. Will the holdings that are converted be in terms of bibliographic items and/or express discrete physical items?

4. What standards and formats will be employed?

Conversion of holdings on a physical piece basis is extremely time consuming and tedious. Nevertheless, it is absolutely essential to holdings at the item level if a system is intended to support circulation and inventory control. A complicating factor here is that, unlike the holdings data content standards that were described earlier, there are no national standards for the machine-readable *format* for communicating holdings data at any level for any type of material. Work on this subject is in progress and is urgently required as more and more libraries are involved in conversion and are attempting to exchange and share data in machine-readable form.

In the 1980s standards for library automation as a whole have moved into the spotlight. The lack of standards can lead to chaos in automated systems.[16] Further, the lack of standards means that there will be many groups attempting to devise standards and formats appropriate to serials holdings statements, among other types of holdings, and further confusion will result.

The lack of accepted formats is another one of the problems associated with converting holdings data concurrently with bibliographic data. This is particularly true if conversion is done through a bibliographic utility. For example, in an OCLC record holdings data are ordinarily converted in the 049 field or the 590 field of a bibliographic record. In many cases it has proven more effective to enter complicated holdings directly into a local system. Union list or summary level holdings present additional options, most noticeably on OCLC.

HOLDINGS CONVERSION TO SUPPORT UNION LISTING

Union lists were one of the earliest uses of machine-readable serial records, dating back to the 1960s. Some libraries often made available lists of just the titles they currently receive. They left comprehensive serials holdings to other listings, such as the catalog or serials records. Whether lists of serials holdings were for one library, different libraries within one institution, or a cooperating group of libraries on a local, state or regional basis, these were among the first applications of data processing and conversion of data in libraries.

Lack of Standards

Many serials union lists often contained very brief holdings statements. In some cases, these did not go beyond an indication of the institutions that held some or all of the titles. Failing any other "standard" for holdings statements, many union lists tried to follow the holdings statement format found in *Union List of Serials* and *New Serial Titles*. These did not provide for differentiating portions of holdings in microform. Many libraries adopted the convention of indicating microform by (M). Others spelled out the words MICROFILM or MICROFICHE. Again, because there were no standards and also because the data were converted for local use only, many different formats evolved for holdings. They included an almost infinite variety of levels of detail in the content of the holdings statements.

ANSI Standard

Finally in 1980 an important step was made in standardizing the data content of summary level serials holdings statements with the adoption of the ANSI standard.[17] This specifies three levels for recording summary holdings. Level 1 encompasses the Location Data area, which requires the code for the institution that holds the item. Level 2 includes the General Holdings Data area. This area contains coded data on the date of report, completeness of published run, acquisitions status, nonretention and any local notes. Level 3 contains specific holdings information. As mentioned before, this information has sometimes been entered in a field in the bibliographic record. In OCLC it can also be entered in a local data record in the serials control subsystem in two fields designed specifically to communicate union list information, Summary Copy Holdings Display (SCHD) and Summary Institution Holdings Display (SIHD).

OCLC's Union Listing

OCLC's union listing capability was originally developed as a result of funds made available from an HEA Title II-C grant awarded to Indiana University (see Wittorf).[18] It has gained widespread interest and as of December 1982 at least 26 union list groups had been profiled by OCLC to participate in union listing.

It is no exaggeration to say that much of the serials data conversion taking place in the early 1980s is for the purpose of participation in OCLC's union listing. This listing will undoubtedly continue to grow in popularity as its effectiveness as an online resource for interlibrary loan and collection management continues to be demonstrated. In addition, OCLC is planning offline products from its union listing capability. These will include printed or COM fiche products for either individual institutions or all members of a union list group. A tape for a union list group as a whole will be available to the designated union list agent. Customized products for subsets of a group can then be produced.

In creating holdings records for union listing on OCLC or on any other union list, a bibliographic record or citation must first be identified. As discussed above, one major decision concerns successive title versus latest title cataloging. Another consideration relates to serials titles held wholly or in part in microform. Both the *ANSI Standard for Serial Holdings Statements at the Summary Level* and *AACR2* specify separate records for print and microform representations of a work. OCLC states a preference for adhering fully to the standards, and many union list groups including the Pennsylvania Union List of Serials have made the decision to create separate bibliographic and holdings statements for each format.[19,20]

Other groups have adopted the alternative allowed by OCLC of putting holdings for microforms in the note subfield of the holdings statement for the print copy. This is because most users are primarily concerned with the content of the work and not its format. Therefore, they prefer that all holdings for a title display together rather than requiring separate searches, as is presently the case on OCLC and most other systems.

One of the important features of OCLC's union listing capability is that it will accept holdings for libraries that are not OCLC cataloging participants. This makes it possible to continue and expand traditional regional or state union lists, whether a library participates in another bibliographic utility or participates in none at all. It should also be noted that conversion of holdings into local data records on OCLC can serve two purposes. The OCLC Serials Control Subsystem, of which local data records are part, also provides the capability of check-in of serials and, eventually, of claims or binding control. Thus, one data conversion effort including creation of a local data record provides the base for other applications. The same is true in other systems, including online remote access serials management systems maintained by serials subscription vendors such as Faxon.[21]

RECLASSIFICATION IN CONJUNCTION WITH CONVERSION

If a library collection needs to be reclassified, for example, from Dewey to the Library of Congress (LC) Classification, it can be cost-effective to combine reclassification with data conversion. With one access of a source data base, a library can create a machine-readable record for each title in its collection, and, if desired, can order cards with new classification numbers. Combining both efforts is particularly effective because, using a bibliographic utility or another source of MARC records, a library can normally find two or more classifications in any single online record. Virtually all reclassifications conform to the LC Classification system.[22] Therefore, an online data base that has most records with an LC number is invaluable in a reclassification project.

Reclassification in conjunction with conversion is further facilitated by the ability to print book labels from the machine-readable records. Thus a library, in one operation, can convert its bibliographic and holdings data to machine-readable format, reclassify the publications and print appropriate labels. A library that may not have classified its periodicals previously can now consider undertaking a classification project for the first time (see Carter).[23] Without the conversion of the necessary data to machine-readable format and the capability this provides for the automated assistance to technical processing, such an undertaking would not be feasible in most cases.

A similar project is changing the subject headings in a library's bibliographic records from one list of subject headings to another. Grosso described manual conversion of a catalog from the *Sears List of Subject Headings* to the *Library of Congress Subject Headings*.[24] This type of project ideally could be done at the time of the conversion from a manual to a machine-readable catalog. Grosso cites the widespread availability of automated cataloging with the presence of LC subject headings as a major factor in a conversion to the LC subject headings. The prospective conversion of a library's cataloging can proceed more rapidly by accepting records with LC headings than by making the machine-readable records match the subject headings on the library's shelflist record.

TREATMENT OF PRE-*AACR2* RECORDS

All libraries attempting to convert bibliographic records to machine-readable form in the 1980s must confront the presence of *AACR2*. There are three major areas of potential conflict between records cataloged in accordance with *AACR2* and those cataloged in accordance with previous cataloging codes. They are:

1. Form of name used in a heading (personal, corporate, conference, uniform title or series);

2. Choice of access points;

3. Description, including punctuation.

By far the most critical, at least in application in most locally oriented machine-based systems, is the form of name. Most of the following discussion will focus on the form of name problems.

Authority Control

The issue of which of several possible names to use is closely tied to the question of authority control. For example, cataloging rules preceding *AACR2* called for the entry of a person under the fullest form of his or her name, such as "David Herbert Lawrence." In contrast, *AACR2* specifies that the commonly used form of the name should be the established heading, with qualifiers for the full form, if known. In the case cited, "Lawrence, D.H. (David Herbert)" becomes the entry form.

Another noticeable difference between *AACR2* and earlier rules occurs in corporate names. Previously the rules for formulating corporate names often required that the direct form of the name be preceded by the city in which the corporate body is found. For example, the old entry form for "Center for Research Libraries" was: "Chicago. Center for Research Libraries." The new rules call for entry directly under "Center for Research Libraries."

Depending on the number of search keys in a machine system and the specifics of the search keys, a user of a machine catalog may or may not find all relevant or related entries that are actually present in the data base being searched. It is particularly important that a searcher can have confidence that all entries relevant to his or her access terms have been retrieved (see Malinconico and Fasana).[25] In the card catalog, this problem was ordinarily solved by a cross-reference structure that was syndetic in nature and part of an authority system. A syndetic structure is one which ties together related items, and those that are either more general or more specific than a particular item.

An authority control system selects an authoritative heading for each entity and provides appropriate references to it from variant forms. Without consistency in headings, bibliographic searches of a catalog may not retrieve all works by one author or versions of the same work (see Schmierer and Runkle).[26,27] On the other hand, as Runkle noted, the need for a coherent display has not been proven.

Form of Name

As discussed above, a library must decide on any standards it wants to employ regarding form of name and on whether to use a source data base that has only *AACR2* forms or mostly *AACR2* forms of names. However, in most cases, the library's own catalog records will contain names formulated under a variety of cataloging rules. Therefore, it must answer these questions: Should it make all names in the machine-readable records match the names in its own catalog record? Should it accept whatever form of name is found in a matching record in a source data base? Or should it convert all forms of names to *AACR2* (or the form in any subsequent standard that might exist at the time of a conversion effort)? Answers will depend upon the library's long-range plans for authority control and upon the basic purposes for which the converted data will be used.

If the purpose of the data conversion is to participate in a union list of serials, it may not be critical to update forms of name or choice of entries. Union lists are compiled over a period of time and individual participants may handle any particular publication quite differently in terms of entry in local records.[28] Therefore, there is no way a union list entry can match the local entry maintained by each of its participants.

In this sense, union lists or other "union" catalogs serve primarily as finding or location tools. The catalog for a single library, however, is its major research tool. Therefore, integrity within the individual catalog is important and the user should find related works grouped together.

Subject Headings

Given the fact that forms of headings vary widely between *AACR2* and pre-*AACR2* rules, it is especially important to consider how variant forms can be brought together. Although not an *AACR2* issue, the topic of subject headings is related. There are three options for bringing together subject headings:

1. Upgrade the heading at the time of conversion;

2. Provide in an automated system the capacity of making global changes on a one-by-one basis;

3. Wait for a full online authority system and reference structure, which can make transparent to the user the variation in terms through the retrieval of all related. items.

Any approach requires tradeoffs.

Option 1, upgrading a heading at the time of conversion, may improve the situation for the user at an early stage but it may slow down a conversion effort. Option 2, which calls for global changes, will slow the process of making the catalog effective for the users, but will keep conversion speed up and costs down. This approach was used by the Hennepin County (MN) Library when it did its retrospective conversion. It undertook its initial conversion "without mechanical control or systematic attempt at recataloging."[29] The first conversion was hindered by almost 50 years of variation in cataloging practices. Hennepin County upgraded its records by running its converted bibliographic file against the authority file of the New York Public Library.

The third solution for the authority problem is an online comprehensive syndetic authority structure that can be programmed to be transparent to users. An online authority system is the long-term goal of many systems. However, most libraries planning conversion projects must realize that it is in the future (five or more years) and that the library can expect only partial satisfaction on the part of its users in the interim.

BAR CODING OR OTHER INDIVIDUAL ITEM CONTROLS

Bar coding or OCR labeling have been discussed in Chapter 3 from the viewpoint of where in the conversion process machine-readable labels should be added. The topic is briefly discussed in this chapter primarily for the purpose of reviewing some of the labeling options. As has been stated earlier, bar codes are only one type of individual item controls that are machine readable. Another option is magnetic strips, which might be used on patron badges.

Machine-readable bar code labels to support automated circulation systems were first introduced in England in 1972. They made their first appearance in the United States in 1974, and required two different varieties of light pens to be read. Most bar code labels have a numeric control number, of which one digit may be a check digit and several digits may provide an institution identifier. A code for type of label, e.g., library item or patron identifier, may also be built into the bar code. A bar code label has patterns of bars printed on it that are read into the machine system. They may also contain an eye-readable rendering of the numbers in the bar code. Some libraries have included the call number with which the label is identified.

The National Library of Medicine has gone beyond a label with bar coding.[30] The item identifier label it has selected includes both a bar coded number and that same number in eye-readable form in an OCR readable type. Because OCR has been considered to hold the most promise for the future, it is wise to select a label that can be read by either method.[31] As Rice stated, OCR technology can be expected to improve greatly within the next few years. Therefore, for a relatively small additional cost, the initial selection of a label that includes the representation of the identifier in both bar code and OCR can keep a library's options open.

Compatibility of Labels

The issue of how to keep options open can be a factor in the timing of the selection of a machine-readable label. A library may commit itself to retrospective and/or prospective data conversion either for circulation purposes or to support a future integrated or linked system. However, it may not have yet selected its automated system. De Klerk commented: "Librarians considering bar coding, prior to selecting an automated system, will be concerned about compatibility of the bar codes with the system they eventually choose, both as regards scanning equipment and system software."[32] She reported that, fortunately, most devices that read one type of bar code need only slight modification, if any, to read other types of bar codes.

Furthermore, software can accommodate differences in codes. With that in mind, Carnegie-Mellon University Libraries selected the Codabar label available through Data Composition, Inc. in advance of selecting its automated system.[33] By beginning conversion of its shelflist and also labeling new acquisitions, Carnegie-Mellon planned to avoid the necessity of calling up the records a second time in order to enter bar code information.

Content of the Label

In selecting the machine-readable label, it should be remembered that the item identifier becomes an integral part of the data base. As was stated in Chapter 2, the data base can be expected to outlast any particular system in which it is first used. Therefore, it is very important to think ahead when selecting item identifier labels. Consideration should be given to the content of a label as well as to the type of label, as discussed above. For example, it will be necessary to decide whether the institutional identifier will be general to the institution or whether it will identify different elements of it, such as various branch or departmental libraries. A patron identifier may serve only to distinguish patron data from library data or it may attempt to identify the type of patron, such as faculty or staff, juvenile borrower or library trustee. These initial decisions will be part of a system for a long time. They will affect, among other things, the depth of detail that may be possible in analyzing growth and use of a collection.

Costs of Labeling

A library should not be overly concerned about saving money on the labels. Compared to the cost of applying the labels and entering the information into the data base, the cost of the label itself is negligible. Bar code label prices vary based on several factors, including size, lamination, inclusion of eye-readable representations, and quantity ordered. For example, bar code labels without lamination may cost approximately $18.00 per thousand if 50,000 are ordered to $16.25 per 1000 if 500,000 are ordered. They may cost even less if the library purchases special equipment and produces its own labels. In item controls, as in all other aspects of data conversion, decisions must be made that provide for the future as well as the present.

SUMMARY

All of the factors discussed in this chapter can present special problems and can have long-term implications for the content of and access to a machine-readable data base. The four areas covered here—conversion of serial records, reclassification in conjunction with conversion, treatment of pre-*AACR2* records and bar coding or other individual item controls—are not the only areas needing special consideration. In some libraries, audio-visual materials, for instance, would require close consideration. However, those highlighted above are encountered most frequently.

Serials Conversion Issues

Conversion of serial records has been an area of intense activity on a nationwide basis in the last decade. Because of the CONSER project, many libraries will find that most serials titles they hold already have a record in machine-readable form. However, some of the records will have been converted in accordance with earlier cataloging rules, specifying entry of all title changes for related publications under the latest title. *AACR2* specifies successive entry for serials, which requires a separate bibliographic record for each title change. Many machine-based systems are designed to best handle successive entry records.

In conversion of serials, complications arise from the variations in cataloging practice mentioned above. Many such conversions will require putting some or all of the holdings for each serial title in machine-readable form. Libraries must decide whether or not to identify holdings with each separate title change. In addition, they must decide whether to enter them into a source data base at the time of conversion of the bibliographic data, or to reserve the conversion of holdings for a local system. Most important, serials holdings lack a standard format for their machine-readable communication.

To date there has been a widespread implementation of the *ANSI Standard for Serial Holdings Statements at the Summary Level.* It has caught on in part because it is required in OCLC's union listing capability, which has become widespread. As offline products from the OCLC union listing become available, even more users should be attracted to it. The OCLC union listing capability has already been responsible for much serials data conversion, both bibliographic and holdings. This should continue, and the OCLC list may indeed become a de facto national union list. It will be one of many reasons for data conversion of serial records, along with the desire to provide better control over serial records.

Reclassification Issues

Reclassifying a collection when it is converted may be another special consideration in data conversion. Because it is relatively cost-effective, a number of libraries have attempted this. Upgrading or converting subject headings from one standard to another is also a possibility.

Every conversion project must deal with records cataloged prior to the introduction of *AACR2.* Some may convert headings into a pre-*AACR2* form while others may elect to put all headings into *AACR2* form as they are converted. If the former option is chosen, a library will need to provide for some type of authority structure: new entries will use current forms and these must be linked to previously used variations of the same name or the user may miss relevant items. While some authority work has been done in connection with automated systems, in general, sophisticated authority systems to support online library files, such as a catalog, are not available. Because an online machine-readable authority structure is not readily available, it is helpful for data conversion projects to enter as many data as possible in conformance with current standards.

Identification Issues

When data conversion's purpose is to support circulation and/or inventory control, a machine-readable label that uniquely identifies each item is usually attached to the item. The identification number for each item is then entered in the data base. The two most common types of labels are bar codes and OCR labels, although labels are available that combine both. Where possible, combination labels should be selected. This will give the library maximum flexibility in adapting to future technological changes.

This chapter has identified a few of the most commonly encountered special considerations involved in data conversion. Chapter 5 will examine the methods of conversion in more detail.

NOTES

1. Michael Gorman, "The Current State of Standardization in the Cataloging of Serials," *Library Resources & Technical Services* 19(4): 301 (Fall 1975).

2. Ibid.

3. Ruth C. Carter, "Playing by the Rules—*AACR2* and Serials," in *Serials Management in an Automated Age* (Westport, CT., Meckler Publishing, 1982), 11-29.

4. Richard Anable, "The Ad Hoc Discussion Group on Serials Data Bases: Its History, Current Position and Future," *Journal of Library Automation* 6(4): 207 (December 1973).

5. "Now, Add CONSER to your Conversation," *American Libraries* 8(1): 21-22 (January 1977).

6. Richard Anable, "CONSER: Bibliographic Considerations," *Library Resources & Technical Services* 19(4): 341 (Fall 1975).

7. Ibid., 341-342.

8. *American National Standard for Serial Holdings at the Summary Level,* ANSI Z39.42—1980 (New York: American National Standards Institute, 1980).

9. "Draft Proposed American National Standards for Serial Holdings Statements at the Detailed Level" (Washington, DC: American National Standards Committee Z39, 1982).

10. Margaret McKinley, "A Pragmatic Approach to Serials Data Conversion," *Serials Review* 7(1): 85 (January/March 1981).

11. Harry H. Kamens, "OCLC's Serial Control Subsystem: A Case Study," *Serials Librarian* 3(1): 43 (Fall 1978).

12. Ibid., 43-55.

13. Nancy Melin Buckeye, "The OCLC Serials Subsystem: Implementation Implications at Central Michigan University," *Serials Librarian* 3(1): 31-42 (Fall 1978).

14. William J. Willmering, "Online Centralized Serials Control," *Serials Librarian* 1(3): 243-249 (Spring 1977).

15. Tom W. Harrison and A. Patricia Miller, "On-line Interactive Serials Management at Marathon Oil Company," *Journal of Library Automation,"* 12(3): 283-289 (September 1979).

16. "Standards Gain Stature as Automated Systems Multiply," *American Libraries* 13(8): 522 (September 1982).

17. *American National Standard.*

18. Robert Wittorf, "ANSI Z39.42 and OCLC," *Serials Review* 6(2): 87-92 (April/June 1980).

19. OCLC, *Serials Control: Users Manual: Addendum 1. Union Listing Capability* (Revised May 1981).

20. Ruth C. Carter, "Cataloging Decisions on Pre-*AACR2* Serial Records from a Union List Viewpoint," in *Union Lists: Issues and Answers* (Ann Arbor, MI: Pierian Press 1982), 77-80.

21. "On-line Serials Check-In Service Designed by Faxon," *Journal of Library Automation* 13(3): 207 (September 1980).

22. Robert L. Mowery, "The 'Trend to LC' in College and University Libraries," *Library Resources & Technical Services* 19(4): 389-397 (Fall 1975).

23. Carter, "Playing by the Rules," 11-29.

24. Katherine Thompson Grosso, "Converting a Catalog from Sears Subject Heading to Library of Congress Subject Heading," *Illinois Libraries* 62(7): 631-633 (September 1980).

25. S. Michael Malinconico and Paul J. Fasana, *The Future of the Catalog: The Library's Choices* (White Plains, NY: Knowledge Industry Publications, 1979), pp. 35-36.

26. Helen F. Schmierer, "The Relationship of Authority Control to the Library Catalog," *Illinois Libraries* 62(7): 599-602 (September 1980).

27. Martin Runkle, "Authority in On-line Catalogs," *Illinois Libraries* 62(7): 603-606 (September 1980).

28. Carter, "Cataloging Decision on Pre-AACR2 Serial Records," 77-80.

29. Malinconico and Fasana, 38.

30. National Library of Medicine, "Request for Proposal for: Labeling Collection with Machine-Readable Identifiers (MRI)," RFP number NLM-81-108/DHE, attachment A, p. 7 (August 20, 1981).

31. James Rice, "OCR for Libraries: Only a Few Years Away," *Library Journal:* 1603-1605 (September 1981).

32. Ann de Klerk, "Barcoding a Collection—Why, When and How," *Library Resources & Technical Services* 25(1): 84 (January/March 1981).

33. Ibid., 84.

5
Comparison of Data Conversion Methods

Traditionally, any large and complex project, be it data conversion or the building of a new library—or, indeed, the construction of a sewer line—requires consideration of three elements: time, cost and performance. In addition, any such project needs careful planning if it is to be executed successfully. The planning considerations for data conversion have been discussed in earlier chapters. There are several ways to carry out this effort. In some situations cost is the most important consideration. In others—for example, if a new circulation system is to begin operation next year—time might override cost factors. In yet other cases the quality of the data base might be the most important factor.

This chapter describes and compares different conversion methods. It examines the factors of time and quality, and discusses the staff considerations pertinent to each approach. The chapter includes a worksheet (Figure 5.1) which will help managers both analyze the cost factors of each method and prepare a budget for whichever alternative is chosen.

BASIC METHODS

The basic methods for a data conversion effort are:

1. An in-house approach in which the conversion is added to the regular work flow;
2. An in-house approach which adds special project staff;
3. Conversion by an agency outside the library.

Each approach will be examined in terms of its advantages and disadvantages; the type of personnel required; and the level of skill or training the project personnel need. (The reader is also referred to Chapter 3 for a discussion on essential data conversion skills and training.) An analysis of cost factors will follow.

ADDING CONVERSION TO REGULAR WORK FLOW

This approach allows for the greatest amount of control by the library manager and, as such, has the highest probability of producing a quality product. While it probably will not add new costs to the overall budget, it is the most labor-intensive approach (in terms of demands on existing staff) for a library to take. It also has the highest probability of never being completed.

Advantages and Disadvantages

Combining conversion with the regular work flow minimizes new costs while maximizing the performance of the personnel on hand. It is the approach that libraries often took a decade ago. There are a number of positive aspects to this approach:

1. Since regular library staff are employed, project personnel will not require much additional training;

2. Since conversion staff will be using the product after it is completed, they may exercise more quality control;

3. If work flow is uneven, personnel can move between the project and their regular work;

4. Personnel will be familiar with the input documents, and with any irregularities or special needs of the library;

5. There will be no need to remove input documents from the library;

6. The project can be done within the library's current personnel budget.

The overriding disadvantage of this approach is the length of time it will take to complete. A useful product probably will not be available for several years, and as the project drags on, both the quality of the work and staff morale will suffer.

Staff Considerations

Adding conversion to the regular work flow involves library personnel at all levels. Additional supervisory duties will be added to the normal work load of department heads, associate directors and the library's chief administrative officer. While current staff, usually technical services personnel, can add conversion to their regular tasks, their work hours may have to change if the library uses a bibliographic utility that provides significant price breaks for evening and weekend hours (see Chapter 6). The change in work hours may also extend to supervisory personnel.

In general, it is not advisable to have data entry personnel work more than three consecutive hours at a terminal. With this conversion approach, other library duties can provide a break from the straight inputting task.

If an inventory is included as part of the data conversion effort, it will be the project's most labor-intensive aspect, depending on the size of the institution. To accomplish the inventory within a reasonable period of time, the library will either have to assign all staff to this project during a vacation period, or it will have to use part-time labor, such as from work-study or summer employment programs.

ADDING SPECIAL STAFF

While this approach allows a fair degree of control (since the project is still in-house), it often creates more difficult management problems. However, this method also increases the chances for a conversion project to be successfully completed within a reasonable time frame.

Advantages and Disadvantages

There are a number of advantages to adding special staff:

1. Control of the project remains with the library;

2. There will be no need to remove input documents from the library;

3. Permanent staff will be relieved of much of the conversion workload—however, major cataloging problems, such as foreign language materials, may be left for cataloging personnel;

4. The project will probably be completed within a reasonable time, since special staff are dedicated to the conversion project (i.e., have no other library duties).

There are also some negative aspects to this approach:

1. It is harder to provide adequate quality control measures;

2. Extra supervisory personnel will be needed—either staff librarians or outside personnel;

3. Additional physical space and equipment may be needed;

4. The project will probably have a high turnover rate, since most of the personnel are hired on a part-time basis;

5. Costs will increase.

Staff Considerations

Unlike the first method discussed, adding a new workforce for the conversion effort introduces a new set of recruitment, training, supervision and scheduling problems. In many cases, libraries have hired people who have some familiarity with cataloging records—library school students or others with a library background—for the conversion project. The number of people hired varies with the scope of the project and the number and type of records to be converted. Typing skills and accuracy are generally more important than speed or familiarity with data processing.

A training program should be designed for the new staff. If trained properly, these project staff members can move into regular library positions when and if such positions become available.

Since the new personnel will be unfamiliar with the library and its operation, adequate supervision is essential. An on-site supervisor for every four to five data entry personnel will make the project run smoothly. In some libraries, outside librarians are hired as supervisors. In others, a staff librarian—usually from the technical services department and preferably with a cataloging background—is designated. Along with supervision, a procedures manual is necessary, to ensure continuity and maintain quality—especially in light of the high turnover rate that can be expected.

As with the first approach, personnel inputting records should work at terminals no more than three to four hours at a time. (If more than two consecutive hours are spent at the terminal, some break time should be provided.) If it is necessary for them to work for longer periods of time, perhaps they can take on other duties, such as bar code labeling or inventory, to limit the amount of time spent at the terminal.

USING AN OUTSIDE AGENCY

An outside agency can convert the data off-site, away from the library, or it can bring its own personnel into the library and do the conversion on-site.

Advantages and Disadvantages

The benefits of contracting with an outside agency for off-site conversion are:

1. Under contract, the costs can be predefined;

2. The time it takes to complete the conversion can be more precisely estimated, and penalties for late delivery can be included in the contract;

3. An experienced agency can be more cost-efficient than the library staff;

4. An outside agency can help the library manager plan, as well as conduct, the conversion.

There are some negative aspects, however:

1. There will be more direct out-of-pocket costs;

2. There is much less opportunity to review performance and work quality;

3. Representations of the shelflist, i.e., either the shelflist cards themselves, or a microfilm of the cards, may have to be sent outside the library.

An on-site conversion by an outside agency would have all of the benefits listed above, with one major addition: input documents (or representations of them) would not have to be sent outside the library. The drawbacks to this method include:

1. More direct out-of-pocket costs would be incurred;

2. Although the work is performed in-house, it is still difficult to review the quality of the work done;

3. Extra physical space and/or equipment may be needed;

4. There is the possibility that agency project staff will conflict or interfere with on-going library processing.

If the library is using an outside agency, whether for off-site or on-site conversion, choosing a reliable vendor is of utmost importance. Chapter 6 will offer guidelines on how to select a vendor and what to require in a contract.

COSTS

The costs of a data conversion project depend not only on the method chosen—in-house or outside agency—but on many other factors as well. These include the scope of the conversion project; the number and type of records to be converted; the standards used for the data conversion; the number of personnel on hand and their expertise in this area; what type of equipment the library has, and what type it needs to lease or purchase; telecommunications charges; and much more.

Depending on the data conversion method selected, not all costs will show up as additional out-of-pocket costs to the library; for example, salaries of regular staff would not be new or additional costs. Nevertheless, for planning and budgeting purposes, it is important to identify all expenses in order to calculate the actual cost to the library of the data conversion project. It will be important to determine which costs will be covered by the library and what additional funds must be secured.

The many variables associated with a data conversion effort make it impossible to suggest what the costs of any particular method will be. However, a conversion manager can make an accurate estimate if he is aware of all the cost elements that must be considered. Using the worksheet shown in Figure 5.1, the manager will be able to reasonably assess the unit (per record) and total costs of the conversion project. In addition, the worksheet will assist the manager in selecting the most appropriate method for accomplishing the project. The following section defines the terms on the worksheet and explains how to use it.

82 DATA CONVERSION

Figure 5.1 Data Conversion Cost Analysis Worksheet

Method being evaluated (check one): ☐ In-house, add to work flow   ☐ In-house, special staff   ☐ Contract out

Project Stages \ Elements	Project Definition and Decision	Inventory	Bibliographic or Other Item Data Conversion	Bibliographic or Other Item Data Problem Resolution	Patron Data Conversion	Patron Data Problem Resolution	Authority Files Construction	Initial Project Evaluation	File Maintenance	Totals
Data base costs including network fees										
Equipment (1) data base access										
Purchase										
Lease										
Maintenance										
Other service fees										
Equipment (2) data capture/interface										
Purchase										
Lease										
Maintenance										
Other service fees										
Financing costs										
Institutional overhead										

Figure 5.1 Data Conversion Cost Analysis Worksheet (cont.)

Project Stages Elements	Project Definition and Decision	Inventory	Bibliographic or Other Item Data		Patron Data		Authority Files Construction	Initial Project Evaluation	File Maintenance	Totals
			Conversion	Problem Resolution	Conversion	Problem Resolution				
Personnel										
Administrator's cost										
Supervisor (librarian)										
Team leader(s)										
Data entry clerks										
General assistants										
Clerical										
Consultants										
Postage/freight/insurance										
Space										
Supplies										
Tape product										
Telecommunications										
Telephone										
Vendor/contract cost										
Totals										

HOW TO USE THE WORKSHEET

It is important to keep in mind that a separate worksheet should be used for each general approach, and for each additional variable, such as time or quality. (For example, a manager may want to figure the cost of an in-house/add more work project spread over two years, then over four, etc.; or, the cost of a two-year project using less expensive equipment, less experienced staff, etc.)

For those persons familiar with microcomputer spreadsheet programs such as "VisiCalc," it becomes obvious that an analysis of interdependent variables such as these can be aided by such a tool. The worksheet was specifically designed to be compatible with such analysis programs.

Elements

In alphabetical order on the left hand side of the worksheet are the individual components (Elements) that make up the total time, quality and financial costs of a project. The cost of an element can be fixed without regard to number of units or records (for example, some equipment costs), or it can be a step function (for example, one piece of equipment will handle up to a maximum of so many units). In some cases the cost is directly related to a unit (for example, certain data base royalties such as a first time use charge), and in other cases it is a percent of another cost or subtotal (for example, financing cost). In some instances, an element may not be applicable (for example, institutional overhead).

Project Stages

The columns running across the top represent the Project Stages. These stages have been discussed in detail in previous chapters and therefore will not be reviewed here. It is important to note, however, that the columns "Bibliographic or Other Item Data" and "Patron Data" have been divided into two sections: "Conversion" and "Problem Resolution." These refer to items that are converted but are later found to have some problem (as a result of an error check), or that could not be converted on the first pass. Such items, though they may be relatively few, usually require the attention of higher level personnel and therefore can represent a considerable expense.

Data Base Cost Including Network Fees

Data base providers charge fees related to the use of the record, usually expressed in unit costs. In some cases, regional networks add a surcharge to these fees for their local documentation, training and accounting services. To determine this cost, multiply the estimated number of records by the unit charge, add any surcharge and place the total in the appropriate column (most likely Bibliographic or Other Item Data: Conversion).

Equipment (1) Data Base Access

The four items included here—purchase, lease, maintenance, other service fees—relate to obtaining equipment specifically for access to a vendor's data base. To determine costs, the purchase (or lease) price is multiplied by the number of machines desired—here too, some vendors assess a surcharge. Any maintenance and service fees must be calculated as well.

Equipment (2) Data Capture/Interface

This section will include the costs for a microcomputer application that might be used either independently or in conjunction with data base access equipment, described above. For example, the library might wish to purchase light pens for use with the data base access equipment, and to lease a microcomputer for the Patron Data Conversion stage. In this case, maintenance fees might be included in the lease rather than incurred (and noted) separately.

In both categories of equipment—data base access and data capture/interface—costs will probably be put not only under the Bibliographic or Other Item Data: Conversion heading, but under many of the other Project Stages as well.

Financing Costs

In a project of this magnitude, the manager must consider the financing costs. In some institutions, the funds will come from outside grants or contracts. In some cases the institution will have to spend institutional funds before the project is implemented and then be reimbursed by the granting or contracting agency. This advance expenditure leads to a real institutional cost which needs to be understood and specified during the initial Project Definition and Decision stage. In many cases a grant or contract can be negotiated so that a significant portion of the money is paid prior to the initiation of the project specifically to cover the start-up costs.

Institutional Overhead

If outside funds are sought, many library administrations require that a percentage of those funds stay at the institutional level to support research offices. In considering the total project cost, particularly if one is looking for outside support, these institutional overhead costs can become quite significant. It often pays to work with the administration to attempt to have these costs waived or reduced.

Personnel

As noted previously, data conversion projects require at least as much internal organization and supervision as any other library project. Therefore, a percentage of the salary of all personnel involved, as well as the salaries of the project staff, must be entered in each appropriate Project Stage column. For example, each project will require the knowledge and supervision of the chief administrative officer of the library. Obtaining outside financial support, dealing with granting agencies in interim reports, working with department heads as functional specifications are designed and other similar tasks all take a significant portion of time and must not be underestimated. Within the technical services department a project supervisor, who may be the department head or assistant head, must be designated.

If a group of data entry clerks are to be working on this project at other than normal business hours those individuals will need an immediate supervisor—noted on these sheets as team leaders—to whom they can take bibliographic and other questions for resolution. In the case of inventory, it would be easy to use all of the personnel now employed by the library full-time on a multi-week project to complete the task. At least in the project definition phase, one may wish to contact a consultant. Costs for all these must be calculated.

Postage/Freight/Insurance

When dealing with an outside contractor for data base conversion, libraries are often led to believe that the unit price quoted is the actual cost. In many cases this quote does not include the provision to the contractor of the data entry forms (the shelflist, or copies of the shelflist). The shipping of these and other related documents to the outside vendor can add a significant cost to a contract price. One should check with various freight forwarders or small package delivery vendors to get an estimate of the shipping costs involved.

Space

Projects that involve a complete inventory and the addition of new equipment and personnel will often require new space. Once the manager has determined that this space can be provided, it is important to determine the cost per square foot.

Supplies

In a complete conversion, one will wish to look at the cost of bar code labels, new spine labels in some cases, new sets of catalog cards, if needed, and general office supplies to support the project.

Tape Product

The product that the conversion effort is producing is a machine-readable record of the bibliographic items converted. As discussed previously, many data base suppliers provide this product on a sliding scale. The cost of the first number of units is quite high, but as one purchases more units per period (e.g., 50,000 units per quarter), the cost per unit drops drastically. In addition to purchasing the tape product, one must be able to store and protect that machine-readable record. In many cases the data base supplier—i.e., the regional network, an outside vendor or a local computer center—will be able to provide exact prices for this element.

Telecommunications

The library's connection to any online data base will include a telecommunications cost. In some pricing schemes the addition of new terminals to an already existing data base will not be an extra cost. In other pricing schemes, the telecommunications charge will be levied per terminal.

Telephone

This element primarily concerns a library that contracts out the work to a vendor. In this case, the library will experience bibliographic conversion problems that must be dealt with, often via long distance telephone calls, at least on a weekly, if not daily, basis.

Vendor/Contract Costs

While this element appears relatively straightforward, as was noted above a unit (per record) price provided by a vendor may not include all the costs associated with the production of those units: postage, freight, insurance, office supplies and duplicating, telephone costs, tape product costs and the like. To get a fair unit price representation under this method, all of those elements must be added to a specified contract price. In addition, the library will continue to have library personnel costs, particularly at the administrative and supervisory level, and—if an inventory is contemplated—at the other levels indicated on the worksheets. Some vendors will provide all of the services including organization and inventory.

Totals

The goal for the financial cost worksheet is to determine a project and a unit (per record) cost. Multiply all cost items by the number of units, except for fixed price items. Add the columns vertically, and then horizontally. Divide the total of the worksheet by the number of units for a fair estimate of the unit costs.

These worksheets do not provide an automatic decision. What they do provide is a method of estimating, with a high degree of accuracy, the comparative costs for a project, allowing a manager to make a decision based on some quantified data. In addition, time and product quality, like money, have an institutional impact and must be assessed. Time and quality are more difficult to quantify than cost. However, simple techniques, such as assigning values from a predetermined scale (high quality=3, mediocre quality=1, etc.) can provide useful information for the worksheets. Consequently, for one data conversion project, a manager should fill out at least three (and as many as nine) worksheets, in order to analyze and compare all the costs of the three basic methods. These worksheets should also allow managers to plan conversion efforts without discovering, halfway through the project, that some important element was not considered.

SUMMARY

The major effort required in data conversion organization is to select an approach, or group of approaches, that answer the library's most important needs. The methods compared in this chapter were in-house with permanent staff, in-house with extra staff and a

88   DATA CONVERSION

contract relationship either on- or off-site. In dealing with a conversion vendor, the amount of in-house work involved will vary considerably. All work may be done outside or a great deal of initial data preparation or entry of search keys to match a source data base may be required by library staff. In almost every case, library personnel will be responsible for review of converted records and frequently will need to resolve problems.

The cost comparison worksheet provided in this chapter will help the project manager select the appropriate conversion method for his or her library. At the same time, the worksheet can be used to budget the entire effort, and to ensure that important elements have not be omitted.

6
Pitfalls

Previous chapters have examined how a library can plan for and conduct a successful data conversion effort. However, much can be learned from data conversion efforts that did not work—from approaches and methods that seemed viable but, for a variety of reasons, failed. This chapter reveals some of the pitfalls of data conversion, drawing on actual cases for the situations it describes.

WHY CONVERSION PROJECTS FAIL

Most of the data conversion projects that have been unsuccessful have had problems in one or more of the following areas: economics, project organization, contracting, data element selection and standardization, and the use of the machine-readable data. Each of these areas will be discussed in turn.

ECONOMIC ISSUES

A number of factors can adversely affect the economics of a data conversion project. Among these are lack of flexibility in the budget, the imposition of new procedures by suppliers after the project is underway and the obsolescence of equipment or methods.

Budgetary Flexibility

With regard to the budget, the manager of a retrospective conversion effort is required to project costs several years into the future. He or she must be careful not to budget exact costs, based on current estimates, since many of these charges may change in the future. Rather, data conversion managers should budget for contingencies, or leave room for unanticipated costs.

Flexibility in the budget is especially important for libraries since they usually receive institutional funding, such as special funding by the legislature for a specific project. These grants usually carry very rigid conditions and terms—for example, if the library has money left over from its allocation for terminals, it cannot normally apply the extra funds to another item which may be over budget. Also, if a major cost surfaces after the budget has been approved and acted upon, it will have serious ramifications for a library in the midst of a conversion effort. An example of this is the data base royalty payment or first time use (FTU) charge, discussed below.

Data Base Use Charges

In the late 1970s, when libraries first began to use OCLC as a source for retrospective data conversion, there was no data base use cost associated with the conversion of records that were already cataloged in the library's collection. For that reason library managers projected a zero cost for use of the OCLC data base for conversion. However, OCLC soon realized that while the conversion of retrospective items helped to build the data base, it also put a strain on the system.

Thus, in order to keep response time and system availability acceptable, OCLC instituted a small data base use cost (five cents per record). While the charge was small to OCLC and small in relationship to the product that was being supplied (a national standard bibliographic record in machine-readable form, edited to suit the needs and requirements of the library in an online environment), that charge raised havoc with budgets that did not include allowance for such a price. In addition, unlike labor, telecommunications and terminal maintenance (which libraries tend to discount, since they are fixed costs and are incurred whether or not a data conversion project exists), the data base use charge was a new line item. As many of the conversion projects were grant funded, there was no allowance in the project budget for this expense.

As of early 1983, that five-cent cost has risen to 22 cents per record for non-prime-time use, and 81 cents for prime-time use. It is to OCLC's credit that the price has been fixed for a defined period (July 1, 1982 through December 1983) at this level to help minimize the problem. However, managers should avoid the pitfall of basing their budgets on the premise that this cost will not rise significantly.

The lessons to be learned here are applicable to projects of any nature: analyze the project budget from all aspects, be particularly cautious of those elements that have value but do not now have a charge associated with them and add flexibility to the budget. In an environment which rewards exact budgeting and also rewards the lowest price, this is not simple to do. But if the project is to have a fair chance of completion, flexibility is essential.

New Work Schedules

The addition of a new charge is one thing; changing the rules for conversion is another. Along with the use charge, OCLC in effect placed a time restriction on the use of its data base for retrospective conversion when it instituted prime-time (weekdays 9 a.m.-4 p.m.) and non-prime-time (weekdays, 7-9 a.m. and 4-10 p.m.; weekends, all day) fees in an effort to level the system load. The substantially higher fees for prime-time use forced libraries to shift conversion projects to non-prime times. This simple change to evenings and weekends created a new and potentially more serious dilemma for the conversion manager: altered work schedules and their attendant personnel problems.

There were instances in which the change in work hours was beneficial to a conversion effort. For example, in a retrospective conversion effort which was dependent on in-house labor, the shift to non-prime time provided a good reason to schedule what might be described as unattractive hours for terminal use. This helped eliminate the excess terminal time capacity that existed in many libraries. However, in most libraries where conversion efforts were underway, this change represented a hardship for managers who suddenly had to schedule personnel into new times, or face a tremendous increase in cost.

In planning current conversion efforts, managers may be able to prevail on existing staff to reschedule their work hours. However, not everyone can or will work nights and weekends, in which case a manager may have to hire part-time personnel. This represents an out-of-pocket cost which may not have been budgeted for, in addition to raising concerns about the quality of the work.

Here again the point to be emphasized is that any assumptions about the stability of external factors should be examined closely. Prudent conversion managers will try to anticipate changes in scheduling or price increases, or at least keep in mind these possibilities. This is especially important since in the near term there will be increasing pressure on all bibliographic utilities to spread the work load over non-prime time, rather than increase their capacities. It is also likely that this will hold true for regular cataloging, as well as retrospective conversion activities.

Managers must keep in mind that conversion projects are often funded through new and outside one-time financial sources, and often bring new and outside elements into all operations of the library. Therefore, questioning assumptions at the beginning of the project and providing as much flexibility as can be afforded will increase the likelihood of successful completion.

Obsolescence of Equipment or Methods

Like budgetary flexibility and new scheduling, obsolescence is a term that is often not well accepted by library governing bodies and some library managers. Yet obsolescence needs to be planned for if the conversion project is to succeed. Obsolescence may be of many kinds. The terminal that is to be moved to a new work site may require rewiring. Certainly the data that must be reconverted because of an improperly designed project the first time are prime examples of highly expensive obsolescence.

Obsolescence can creep into even the best of plans. For example, when OCLC brought out the Model 110 terminal (now discontinued), the TPS light pen that was used to enter bar code data into the record—and which had worked on the older Model 100 and 105 terminals—did not work on the new model. Printers that had specially modified cables to work with older OCLC terminals had to have those cables modified again (back to the standard fortunately) before they would work on the newer OCLC terminals. All of these elements were corrected but, in the meantime, out-of-pocket expenses were incurred and, equally important, time was lost.

If nothing else, this example illustrates that data conversion, unlike many past activities, brings libraries in contact with an industry that is in a state of flux, and for which the rules of time and cost are not easy to forecast. The data processing industry—to which data conversion is wedded—is in a period of dynamic growth. Thus, it is absolutely necessary for data conversion managers to understand and plan for obsolescence and change. As noted previously, librarians will have to educate those who hold the purse-strings, and convince them of the need for change—but in the end it will lead to a much more successful project.

PROJECT ORGANIZATIONAL ISSUES

Even the most well-structured data conversion effort can fall victim to underestimation of the time that actions take. In some data conversion projects, the amount of time needed was underestimated in an effort to reduce costs—and thereby make the project seem more attractive to the funder. However, in data processing it is generally accepted that an action will take three times the amount of time originally estimated. Thus, if you think a project will take one day, plan on three.

Estimating the Time Required

Early in-house conversion efforts estimated that an operator could convert 35 or more records per hour. Often missing from that estimate was consideration of the level of training of the operator, the time lost during retraining, the response time on the system, the amount of editing required to make the record acceptable and the amount of time that the system was available. The literature shows that rates as low as two or three records per hour can occur. For many conversion efforts, however, a rate of approximately 20 records per hour is an acceptable planning figure, assuming minimal editing and assuming an experienced operator.

To estimate time with some degree of accuracy, the manager must sample the records that will be used, analyze the skill levels required for the operators, determine the time that the system will be available, and then add a flexibility factor.

The important concept here is not to take the tendency for underestimation lightly. It easily could be the downfall of the entire effort. The following is an example of a project that failed because of poor time estimates combined with uncontrolled outside factors.

Failure of a Project

In 1980 a number of public libraries in Pennsylvania wrote grants proposals to the State Library of Pennsylvania for federal LSCA funds to support retrospective conversion projects. Based on earlier experiences of time and other costs, these grants were fairly well-designed. In most cases the LSCA funds provided only for OCLC-related costs, but in one case project staff was provided for as well.

The timing of the grant proposal process required that the budget be developed about a year in advance of the start of the project, but the libraries did well in anticipating OCLC's price increases and, based on earlier experience, they provided some flexibility in their estimates. What could not be anticipated, however, was the failure of the OCLC Model 110 terminal and the consequent unavailability of new OCLC terminals from late December 1981 to October 1982.

The library that had budgeted for project staff hired staff in October 1981 to begin the inventory in advance of the conversion effort. A terminal—the first for the library—was scheduled for installation in January 1982 to support the activity of the actual conversion. OCLC instituted a terminal installation freeze, however, which delayed the installation of the terminal for most of the grant period. The grant prohibited carrying the personnel funds forward to the next fiscal year. Thus, the library lost outright most of the conversion effort that it had planned.

Allowing for Unexpected Delays

The technology involved in data conversion brings libraries and their managers in contact with an industry in which there are many variables. The problems of flexibility, obsolescence and other external factors are not new in the business world, but may be new for many libraries. Furthermore, libraries often first encounter these problems when a data conversion effort is undertaken. Dealing with these problems effectively takes new skills and librarians must become knowledgeable about the technology of data conversion not only in order to negotiate with vendors and contractors, but also to educate their governing institutions.

Data conversion managers must bear in mind that it will take a while for staff to become familiar with the effort; that more skills may be required in a staff than first estimated (see Chapter 5); that if a bibliographic utility is used, it will not always be available when needed; that something in the planning stages will go wrong; and that no matter how well-planned a project is, time overruns should always be budgeted for.

CONTRACTING ISSUES

Many of the lessons learned above focus on in-house conversion efforts. It might seem that one way to ensure acceptable performance is to contract the work out to another agency. In this way a fixed price can be negotiated and a set time schedule can be identified. While those are certainly elements of any such contract, there are other elements that a contract should identify.

Various types of agencies will provide off-site data conversion. One type is a bibliographic utility such as OCLC, RLIN or WLN. OCLC now has an extensive staff and makes conversion one of its primary offerings. WLN has a separate retrospective conversion subsystem. Independent contractors are also available. Contractors may use their own data base and may require that the library identify, and in some cases provide, standard numbers associated with the items to be converted in a machine-readable form. Then there are some regional networks that distribute OCLC and provide conversion services for their members (and in some instances for non-members as well). Regional networks may also offer temporary services which provide labor and supervision at the library's site.

Contract Elements

Time and cost per unit can be negotiated with the vendor selected. However, one must be careful to identify any requirements that may seem obvious, but may be subject to interpretation.

In a conversion done off-site, the product is often a machine-readable tape of the converted records. What makes this process difficult is the fact that errors are easy to cover up and hard to detect. Many libraries undertake a conversion effort to make other projects such as an online circulation system or online catalog possible at a later time, but not immediately. How, essentially, does a library manager know that the library has all of the information it is supposed to have on the machine-readable tape, and that it has been done in a manner that is acceptable? Often, a library does not have a machine capable of reading the tape for months or years after its production—yet the vendor is paid upon delivery.

In addition to this work inspection problem, the actual cost elements in the contract need to be examined carefully. A vendor may quote a particular price per record, but may not indicate that there will be a charge for providing a representation of the library's shelflist to the vendor's site. Problems also arise when specifications for conversion forget to include the work that must be done if the record is not in the vendor's data base. Some vendors require the library to provide the data describing the shelflist information in a specific manner—for example, by microfilming the shelflist—and this often requires a tremendous amount of library labor. In essence, unless the specifications are quite explicit, a price that appears to be the lowest per unit may not be, upon more detailed inspection.

Major items to include in the request for proposal (RFP) for an outside service are acceptable time and cost; the provision of a sample tape early in the project, drawn perhaps at random from all of the work done; identification of the record selected from the vendor's data base placed on the library's representation of the shelflist; payment schedules that relate to periodic work done and verified by a third party; and references from the vendor which will provide the library manager with another customer with whom to discuss the quality of the vendor's work.

Choosing a Vendor

While working with an outside source can ensure that a data conversion effort meets time and budgetary requirements, libraries should be very cautious about choosing a vendor. There have been a number of instances where a vendor has bid very low on a project, gotten it, started work on it and tied up the library's money, and then has given up—never having had the capability to do the job adequately in the first place. Then, too, the data processing industry, like other high technology areas, has its share of "fly-by-night" vendors—a phenomenon which libraries may not be used to dealing with.

For these reasons, a library should choose a vendor on the basis of not just the RFP, but on the vendor's good standing with previous customers; his willingness to work with library staff to resolve problems as they occur during the conversion; and his willingness to stand behind the work even after the warranty period has elapsed (which a vendor will do if the library market is very important to him, and not just a sideline).

In addition, a library might be well-advised to contract with an agency with which it has other relationships, rather than with a specialized vendor with which it will have only one dealing (unless the references and reputation of that single-purpose vendor are impeccable). The library is "buying a pig in a poke" and there is often no way around this problem except the goodwill and continuing business relationship of the two parties.

For their part, libraries can write specifications in a manner that allows comparable prices to be obtained, and be willing to pay a little more for an established, reputable vendor. Appendix C lists vendors of data conversion services.

DATA ELEMENT SELECTION AND STANDARDIZATION ISSUES

There are a number of standards that are used for data conversion, including *AACR2* and the machine-readable cataloging standard. However, different levels of quality are permitted even within these standards; for example, *AACR2* permits brief or full notes. Therefore, agreement on data elements, codes and use of fields—not just among technical service staff but among all who will be using the data of a conversion effort—is essential. This may include discussions with representatives from circulation, public services and any other libraries within the conversion project. Inadequate planning in this area often scuttles the plans for online access, circulation systems and resource sharing that many libraries hope to institute once a conversion effort is underway.

In a multicampus library, a public library system, a school district made up of several buildings or a special library serving a corporation with several locations, it is imperative that each inputting element agree upon and follow the same minimal set of input rules. If a group of independent institutions wants to cooperate on a project at some future time— for example, development of an online catalog for a state—this initial standardization is the key that will make the system work or not work.

Permitting Flexibility

Standardization does not mean that every element of local information has to be the same. Certainly, different institutions can have different call numbers for the same item. What is required is that a *range of difference permitted* be identified first and that the rules are followed by all. The rules for data entry are important as the identification of subject headings used. If one library uses a certain symbol in a certain way to mean that a particular portion of the library holds the item, then these symbols have to be known and used in consistent ways by everyone involved in the project. The more consistency there is in the beginning, the easier it will be to make the data merge together for display purposes in the end.

One of the advantages of the MARC record is that it provides a good degree of standardization. Cataloging rules augment this, so that what is available is a standard set of data elements entered in a standard way and with standard machine codes. The records from one MARC-based system can be merged with the records from another such system, but not automatically.

Merging Records

Just as it is well to remember that flexibility is important when budgeting a conversion effort, it is important to recognize that it will take more effort than one might think to merge the records of different institutions. In-depth discussions among data conversion managers regarding the exact methods to be used in the conversion (prior to the beginning of any such effort) will save a tremendous amount of time later. If the conversion effort is to provide, for instance, a statewide data base, then the discussion should take place over the entire state. The results of that discussion need to be formalized into agreements that are ratified by the top management in each library. Samples of the work taken early in the process need to be examined to determine if the process in fact worked. Changes in the process must be communicated to all who are playing by these rules.

Managers should remember that if there is a possibility that two individuals will interpret a seemingly direct statement differently, they will, and this different interpretation will cause difficulties later. Records produced at two different sites probably will not merge at first, and any preliminary sample that can help identify problems will be of the utmost benefit.

DATA BASE MAINTENANCE ISSUES

Although the focus to this point has been on retrospective conversion projects that have made the mass of data machine-readable, there is equal need to examine data base maintenance, or ongoing conversion. Cataloging libraries often skip the procedures so well outlined by them for retrospective work if it appears that the short-cut will save money. There has been more than one library which, when cataloging, has turned to other sources of bibliographic data such as proof slips, and has produced cards from an online bibliographic system only if the card could not be obtained elsewhere.

What is required once the library determines that it is building and maintaining a machine-readable data base is a concentration by all on the maintenance effort that will continue forever. Any change, addition or deletion recorded anywhere must be represented in the data base. Changes in procedures must be documented so that the history of the effort can be recreated if a question arises at a future time. Otherwise, a library will end up facing yet more reconversion a few years later, when it decides to build a data base instead of a card catalog.

USE OF THE MACHINE-READABLE RECORDS

Like anything else, the machine-readable record that represents the converted data can deteriorate. The most extreme case of this occurred when a library completed a comprehensive conversion, only to find that it had no machine-readable record of the effort.

When planning the conversion effort it is essential to make provisions for a machine-readable record of the effort. If the conversion is being done by an outside vendor using his own data base, then the library should require a national standard record that can be exchanged or merged with others. In some cases, unless specified, the record provided is an abbreviated record, which does not have all elements present. Therefore, the product definition should be included in the initial contract. For conversion on one of the major bibliographic utilities, using either the utility, a network, an outside vendor or in-house labor, it becomes more important to be certain that the library will receive a copy of its records when the records are needed.

Obtaining Copies of the Record

The bibliographic utilities provide a price break to the high volume purchaser. Thus, copies of the first 1000 records may cost five cents each, but the next 4000 cost only one cent each, and the next several thousand even less. For this reason, many libraries using OCLC have relied upon their regional network to purchase the combined machine-readable records of all the work of all members in the network. The positive element here is that the cost per record will be less, but the drawback is that the library will not have a copy of the product that it is producing under its direct control.

Records in a machine-readable form, however, require certain maintenance including proper environmental storage, refreshing of the electromagnetic signals on a recurring basis, storage in a security area with storage of a duplicate in another area and the ability to provide the records to the owning library at a cost and in a time frame that meets the library's needs.

Maintaining the Machine-readable Record

In the past little attention has been paid to the care of the product that conversion produces. Some networks and most libraries that used OCLC never purchased the machine-readable records when first available, always assuming that a utility like OCLC would provide them when they were needed. Since the end of the RETROARC project, however, OCLC has not made those records available again. Other bibliographic utilities' customers were more familiar with the concept of using a data base and as a result purchased the tapes when they were made available.

It is important to remember that if the product being produced is a machine-readable record that represents the material in the library's collection, then the project plan must pay serious attention to the provision of the final product to the library. The library, in turn, must pay serious attention to providing an appropriate storage place for the information in that form. Otherwise, the entire conversion effort is wasted.

SUMMARY

A great deal can go wrong in any data conversion effort, but as libraries learn from past mistakes, the odds for success improve. Libraries must guard against the temptation to sacrifice time or money in an effort to make the conversion project more attractive to funders. Conversion managers should allow room in both budgets and schedules for the unexpected—data processing is a new involvement for most libraries, and as with any new technology, there will be a certain amount of trial and error. Most importantly, libraries must decide what it is that they eventually want from the conversion effort, and standardize the input accordingly. Libraries must remember that they are building a data base—not simply producing catalog cards in a more convenient fashion.

This chapter has illustrated some of the pitfalls of data conversion in the hope that managers of future conversion efforts can bypass them. Better still, those contemplating a conversion project should speak to others that have been or are involved in data conversion projects. Appendix A lists more than 200 such libraries, along with a brief description of the type of project they are involved in and whom to contact for further information.

7

Summary and Outlook

Throughout this book, we have stressed the importance of careful planning for data conversion. A successful effort requires a good understanding of the goals and objectives of data conversion, a knowledge of the files to be converted, an understanding of what can be accomplished with available resources, decisions on standards and formats, and consideration of both short- and long-term needs. This book has described applications for machine-readable files. It has identified the steps that should be followed in planning for data conversion, and has provided guidelines for designing a retrospective conversion project and/or maintaining an ongoing conversion effort.

Each data conversion project is different, but we have attempted to cover the key issues and concerns that must be addressed in any conversion effort. It is important to keep in mind that while the retrospective effort might be a *project,* there will always be an ongoing data conversion *process.* Many of the considerations discussed regarding a retrospective conversion project will apply to the ongoing conversion process.

TRENDS IN DATA CONVERSION

A number of trends in data conversion in libraries are apparent at the time of this writing. These include:

- Data conversion is now and will increasingly be encountered in libraries of all types and sizes;

- Sharing resources and participation in cooperative activities continue to be motivating factors in many conversion projects;

- More data conversion is being done to support future integrated automated systems;

- More data conversion of bibliographic records is being done with full records as opposed to the early tendency to convert brief or partial records;

- Adherence to national standards for bibliographic data is widely accepted;

- The need for a standard format for communicating holdings and locations is widely recognized and will receive considerable attention in the next few years.

The list of trends continues with:

- More libraries are at least discussing total retrospective conversion of bibliographic files;

- Patrons increasingly want full records, including subject headings and all of a library's holdings, to be converted to an online catalog;

- The price per record used in a conversion via a major bibliographic utility will steadily increase, but at the same time most records will be found in the utility's data base, thus reducing costs through savings in time;

- Tape management or maintenance of "archive" tapes will be a growing enterprise at least for the next few years; and

- There will probably be more vendors specializing in data conversion.

Data conversion, like other library functions, is benefitting greatly from technological developments, especially in the area of microcomputers and black box interfaces. These allow for direct connections between the bibliographic utilities and the individual library systems, allowing libraries to manipulate the data and thereby save the time and expense associated with using machine-readable tapes.

Using a microcomputer, a library can immediately call up the record, edit it (faster, since each line does not have to be sent for updating), produce the record and have a machine-readable version on hand in the library that can be used to update the circulation record at the same time. Of course, this technique is only acceptable if the library adds the record's symbol to the data base and pays for the record. Otherwise, the library is in breach of its contract with the utility and guilty of unauthorized use of the data.

As the technology becomes more sophisticated, these direct connections will increase—as will the potential for bypassing payment of legitimate charges to the utilities involved. Along with this development—or perhaps in part because of it—the ownership of information in various data bases has been called into question. This issue surfaced dramatically in December 1982, when OCLC announced its intent to copyright its data base. OCLC's action, which copyrights the uniquely arranged and augmented compilation of entries, was undertaken to help prevent unauthorized use. The issue of data base ownership will be the subject of increasing concern and debate in the next few years.

TOWARD INTEGRATED SYSTEMS

As DeGennaro has stated, libraries should do retrospective conversion of their catalogs if they want to speed up automation, improve management and reduce the expense and difficulties of maintaining parallel machine and manual systems.[1] He goes further and specifies a single integrated system incorporating all of a library's bibliographic records as a requirement for taking full advantage of automation. Because network data bases are now very large, complete retrospective conversion is feasible for most libraries. Conversion of bibliographic data has been a very successful nationally cooperative project. Conversion of holdings and other records such as financial and circulation/inventory records are of necessity restricted to the individual library.

It is unrealistic to expect that the description and itemization of all the resources held by libraries will be in machine-readable form. However, a great percentage of these already are converted and more will be. Conversion of records increasingly supports integrated systems within individual libraries and cooperative resource sharing systems through networking and participation in bibliographic utilities. Retrospective data conversion, although often attempted, has only scratched the surface of what is possible for the bibliographic records of the nation's library resources. Prospective data conversion, whether of bibliographic or other records, is by its very nature never completed.

The actual techniques used for data conversion may vary over time, and the systems in which the machine-readable records are used will change as technology changes. However, the need for data conversion will continue and that will require careful planning and adherence to standards. While libraries in the future increasingly will take data conversion for granted, there will always be a need for understanding the principles and concepts involved. We hope we have presented them in this book and that they will be beneficial in future data conversion projects.

NOTES

1. Richard De Gennaro, "Libraries & Networks in Transition: Problems and Prospects for the 1980's," *Library Journal* 106(10): 1047 (May 15, 1981).

Preface to Appendixes

The following three appendixes are directories of libraries with experience in data conversion projects, vendors of conversion services and consultants. The directories were compiled from responses to a questionnaire sent to 408 libraries throughout the country. Of the 242 responses received, 213 were used. (The remaining responses arrived too late for inclusion.)

The following information was requested in the questionnaire: 1) name, address and telephone number of the institution; 2) contact person; 3) name of vendor used, if any; 4) name of consultant used, if any; 5) a brief description of the project and comments of the respondent.

The comments included in Appendix A, the directory of libraries, were made by the contact person named at each institution. Many of the comments note problems encountered and mistakes made during the conversion project. These reports should be particularly useful to libraries that are about to undertake their own projects. The comments are necessarily brief, owing to space limitations, and readers are encouraged to contact the individual named for more detailed information.

The consultants listed in Appendix B are librarians, information specialists or system analysts whose services were used by the libraries surveyed. Likewise, vendors listed in Appendix C are those used by the responding institutions. Further information on consultants and vendors was obtained by follow-up letters and telephone calls.

The lists are by no means complete, nor are the persons, libraries or firms listed recommended or endorsed by the compiler. No claim is made that those included are the only available or qualified participants.

The directory of libraries is organized alphabetically by state and then by the name of the institution. The lists of consultants and vendors are arranged alphabetically by name.

The compiler wishes to thank Elizabeth Fenwick and John Tieberg-Bailie of Northern Illinois University for their assistance.

Elaine Rast
Founders Library
Northern Illinois University
February 1983

Appendix A: Libraries That Have Implemented Data Conversion Projects

ALABAMA

Birmingham Public Library
2020 Park Place
Birmingham, AL 35203
205-254-2551
J. Norfleete Day, Associate Director
Conversion was done on monographs only. Auto-Graphics, Inc. was used.

University of Alabama in Birmingham
Mervyn H. Sterne Library
University Station
Birmingham, AL 35294
205-934-6360
Dr. Jerry W. Stephens, Assistant Director for Administrative Services
Checked shelflist against OCLC data base.

ALASKA

Anchorage Law Library
303 K. St.
Anchorage, AK 99501
907-264-0580
Aimee Ruzicka, State Law Librarian; Laura Bunnell, Technical Services
The Anchorage Law Library's retrospective conversion project involved the Batch Retrospective Conversion Subsystem of WLN. The most rigorous portion of the project was the extensive inventory and weeding that took place prior to the inputting of data.

Kenai Community Library
PO Box 4380
Kenai, AK 99611
907-283-4378
Emily H. DeForest, Librarian
Retrospective information sent to Juneau. Juneau then inputs onto Wylbur, then to WLN. Slow.

University of Alaska, Anchorage
3211 Providence Ave.
Anchorage, AK 99508
907-263-1877
Nancy Lesh, Associate Director in charge of Technical Services
Each record collected on tape in University of Alaska computer network. Then tape sent to WLN, and run against its retrospective conversion data base.

University of Alaska, Fairbanks
Bio-Medical Library
Fairbanks, AK 99701
907-474-7442
Dwight Ittner, Bio-Medical Librarian
The University of Alaska Computer Network has a dual Honeywell 66/40 mainframe time-sharing computer for use by all university personnel and students. This computer is used to create holding tapes that are mailed to WLN.

University of Alaska, Fairbanks
Elmer E. Rasmuson Library
Fairbanks, AK 99701
907-474-7224
Sharon West, Head, Technical Services
Project began immediately upon use of WLN in 1978. Intent is to complete retrospective conversion and eliminate card catalog by the time expansion of facility is completed in late 1984.

ARIZONA

Arizona State Library
Research Library
Department of Library, Archives and Public Records
3rd Floor Capitol
1700 W. Washington
Phoenix, AZ 85007
602-255-4590
Pamela Duett, Head of Technical Services
The law collection was formerly cataloged using a local system of organization (by form, then by author). In August 1981, we began classifying all new legal texts according to Library of Congress K schedules.

Mesa Public Library
64 E. 1st St.
Mesa, AZ 85201
602-834-2726
Peggy Haney, Circulation Librarian
We received a state grant to purchase the MARC tapes in order to pull off the machine-readable data which we modified whenever necessary.

Scottsdale Public Library
3839 Civic Center Plaza
Scottsdale, AZ 85251
602-994-2471
Charline Longstreet, Support Services Manager
Estimated number of titles to be converted was 105,000. AMIGOS searched 105,775 titles and updated 96,177.

Tucson Public Library
PO Box 27470
Tucson, AZ 85726
602-791-4391
Kenneth J. Bierman, Assistant Library Director
Two-hundred thousand titles in CLSI Title Data Base were converted to magnetic tape. Magnetic tape sent to Brodart which searched titles against its MARC data base. Project was very successful.

ARKANSAS

Central Arkansas Library System
700 Louisiana
Little Rock, AR 72201
501-370-5955
Bob Razer, Head of Technical Services
Utilized OCLC to update data base records to reflect CALS shelflist holdings.

COLORADO

Auraria Library
11th and Lawrence
Denver, CO 80204
303-629-2805
Anthony Dedrick, Deputy Assistant Director, Administration
From 1980 to 1983 225,000 titles were entered into the OCLC system, in addition to all current acquisitions from 1980 to the present.

Colorado State University Libraries
Fort Collins, CO 80523
303-491-5911

Irene Godden, Assistant Director for Technical Services
CSUL converted CSU theses and items on water resources to machine-readable format via RLIN as part of this project. OCLC tapes are currently being loaded in the RLIN data base.

Denver Public Library
Technical Services
3840 York St., Unit I
Denver, CO 80205
303-571-2353
Marsha Fralick, Automated Records Department Manager
Retrospective conversion of bibliographic records is done with regular Technical Services staff using either OCLC or the Auto-Graphics Agile II system. Public Service staff enters specific item information to the circulation system (DataPhase) for shelflisting.

University of Denver
Penrose Library
2150 E. Evans
Denver, CO 80208
303-753-3407
Elaine Henjum, Catalog Coordinator
We are converting our present manual card file into machine-readable format by utilizing the OCLC data base. Maintaining a trained staff willing to work at odd hours has been our greatest problem.

CONNECTICUT

Trinity College Library
Summit St.
Hartford, CT 06106
203-527-3151, ext. 302
Jane Willits, Head Cataloger
We chose the in-house (OCLC) rather than vendor method because many of our shelflist cards have less than full cataloging, and we anticipated many problems that could be most easily resolved on-site by access to main catalog or books.

DELAWARE

Wilmington Institute Library
10th and Market Sts.
Wilmington, DE 19801
302-571-7403
Larry L. Manuel, Librarian
Our shelflist containing information on 100,000 titles was packed into boxes provided by OCLC. I was very impressed by the willingness of OCLC to work with us to create a project that was satisfactory to us at an attractive price.

FLORIDA

Florida International University Library
Tamiami Trail
Miami, FL 33199
305-554-2461
Jacqueline M. Zelman, Head, Cataloging Department
Conversion of the Florida International University Library shelflist was begun in November 1975 by the Florida Computer Output Microfiche Catalog (COMCAT) project headed by John Clayton and based in the Orlando (FL) Public Library. A follow-up conversion project was initiated when the North Campus of FIU was added approximately one year later.

Florida State University
Robert Manning Strozier Library
Tallahassee, FL 32306
904-644-5211
J.F. Jones, Assistant Director for Technical Services
Began converting the shelflist of Library of Congress classified materials through OCLC in July 1979.

Jacksonville Public Library
122 North Ocean St.
Jacksonville, FL 32202
904-633-2107
Sylvia Cornell, Head of Catalog Department
Our project was handled by a temporary group of employees (COMCAT Center in Orlando) working on a State of Florida Grant. The coordinator was John Clayton of the Orlando (FL) Public Library. The COMCAT Center used our microfilm to input our cataloging into the OCLC data base.

University of Central Florida Library
PO Box 25000
Orlando, FL 32816
305-275-2564
Margaret Hogue, Systems Librarian
From its beginning, UCF had machine-readable cataloging, but not in MARC format. In 1975, UCF became a member of SOLINET and all cataloging was done through the OCLC system. Since early 1982, we have been adding new records to our circulation system data base (CLSI) through Innovative Interfaces.

University of Miami
Otto G. Richter Library
PO Box 248214
Coral Gables, FL 33124
305-284-3551

Frank Rodgers, Director of Libraries
Conversion of the library's records was made prior to initiation of OCLC cataloging in 1975, using two Apple II microcomputers. Decision to use REMARC was made after two years of matching records against OCLC data base.

University of North Florida
Thomas G. Carpenter Library
St. Johns Bluff Rd., S.
PO Box 17605
Jacksonville, FL 32216
904-646-2550
John M. Hein, Head, Technical Services or Linda Smith, Head Cataloger
The library began retrospective conversion in April 1975, the moment it initiated use of the OCLC cataloging system.

University of South Florida Library
LIB 207
Tampa, FL 33620
813-974-2501
Arthur L. Ketchersid, Assistant Director, Technical Services
The initial conversion effort was begun in 1975 as part of a project funded by the State Library called Florida COMCAT. The USF Library was one of 11 libraries selected to participate in a test of the LAMBDA system developed by SOLINET. Some 410,000 USF records were loaded into the LAMBDA data base and could be searched and maintained online.

University of West Florida
John C. Pace Library
Pensacola, FL 32514
904-474-2457
Jeannie Kamerman, SOLINET Coordinator
Project MERGE (Mechanized Retrieval for Greater Efficiency), the conversion into a machine-readable form of pre-1975 cataloging (the year the institution began cataloging online), was achieved by two data entry operators, two high-level library technicians and one librarian.

GEORGIA

Augusta College
Reese Library
2500 Walton Way (10)
Augusta, GA 30910
404-828-4801
John O'Shea, Assistant Librarian
Shelflist compared to OCLC. Updated if matching. Available clerical staff used on a rotating basis, all hours.

Clayton County Library System
124 Smith St.
Jonesboro, GA 30236
404-478-7120
Carol C. Johnson, Library Director
The project is being done in conjunction with the county government data processing center (IBM equipment). We are using this as an opportunity to weed and upgrade the collections.

Columbus College
Simon Schwob Memorial Library
Columbus, GA 31993
404-568-2042
Callie B. McGinnis, Coordinator of Technical Processing
Enter records for cataloged library materials into the OCLC data base.

Dougherty County Public Library
2215 Barnesdale Way
Albany, GA 31707
912-435-2104
Hal Todd, Director
We did our own work. Our system provides for Coastal Plains Regional Library of Tifton, GA.

Georgia Institute of Technology
Price Gilbert Memorial Library
Atlanta, GA 30332
404-894-4501
Helen R. Citron, Associate Director for Technical Services
In 1965, as a MARC I Pilot Project Library, Georgia Tech started reclassifying and making machine-readable records of its entire collection. The project is still ongoing. We will be completely machine-readable for all holdings when serials and government documents are converted in about five years.

Georgia Southern College Library
Landrum Box 8074
Statesboro, GA 30460
912-681-5115
Kenneth G. Walter, Director
Shelflist is being converted to machine-readable form by inputting into the SOLINET data base by student assistants and clerks working in the evenings.

Lake Lanier Regional Library
275 Perry St.
Lawrenceville, GA 30245
404-963-5231
John Shelton, Director

LC or ISBN number written on approximately 36,000 shelflist cards, and system holdings matched against General Research Corp.'s data base. To date, the project has been very cost effective. Microfiche has been well received by patrons.

Middle Georgia Regional Library
1180 Washington Ave.
Macon, GA 31201
912-744-0850
Charles J. Schmidt, Director
After 18 months our library's in-house conversion of retrospective collection was completed in 1972. The data base products include book catalog, COM-fiche catalog, cataloging and circulation.

Valdosta State College Library
Valdosta, GA 31698
912-247-3244
David L. Ince, Director
OCLC records were examined for consistency with shelflist. Retrospective conversion, LC conversion and COM catalog have been completed on approximately 80% of the collection in the past two years.

HAWAII

Hawaii Department of Education
Office of Library Services
809 8th Ave.
Honolulu, HI 96816
808-732-5571
Masae Gotanda, Head Research and Evaluation Services
The acquisitions-catalog modules were automated in 1976 and 78% of the titles were converted through contract by Blackwell North America. The remainder was converted by the librarians within the system.

IDAHO

Idaho Falls Public Library
457 Broadway
Idaho Falls, ID 83402
208-529-1450
Rena Ferguson, Head, Technical Processing
Converted our brief CLSI records to full records by overlaying them with WLN records. CTI does excellent overlay program.

Lewis-Clark State College
Learning and Resource Center
6th St. and 8th Ave.
Lewiston, ID 83501

208-746-2341
JoAnn Boyd, Department Head, Technical Services
Did conversion through WLN.

Ricks College Learning Resources Center
Rexburg, ID 83440
208-356-2355
Thomas Liau, Head, Technical Services
Before we participated in OCLC we converted our collections into machine-readable form through Blackwell North America. It is much better to do retrospective conversion through OCLC.

University of Idaho Library
Moscow, ID 83843
208-885-6186
Monte L. Steiger, Assistant Director for Technical Services
Matched our shelflist against WLN's data base. Found a little over half. Have 158,000+ in the data base. Have a few over 90,000 left to convert.

ILLINOIS

College of DuPage Learning Resource Center
22nd and Lambert Rds.
Glen Ellyn, IL 60137
312-858-2800, ext. 2280
Robert Veihman, Director of Technical Services and Utilization
By means of OCLC and the Innovative Interfaces system we have completed our conversion of approximately 118,000 titles in a period of 2½ years. We did quality input rather than finding a "hit" and accepting it as is.

Corn Belt Library System
1809 W. Hovey Ave.
Normal, IL 61761
309-452-4485
Henry R. Meisels, Director
Corn Belt Library System entered into an agreement with MARCIVE, Inc. for the production of a machine-readable tape. MARCIVE's hit rate was in the neighborhood of 75%. The project was completed within eight months and the tape was tested. The outcome of the test was satisfactory. We would recommend MARCIVE to libraries engaged in data conversion.

Cumberland Trail Library System
12th and McCawley
Flora, IL 62839
618-662-2679

Nancy Sue Schell, Interlibrary Cooperation Consultant or Pamela Thornton, Technical Services Librarian
CTLS is in the process of going online with a DataPhase ALIS II system.

Deere & Co.
John Deere Rd.
Moline, IL 61265
309-752-4881
Betty S. Hagberg, Manager, Library Services
Convert shelflist to computer readable form using OCLC.

DePaul University Law Library
25 E. Jackson Blvd.
Chicago, IL 60604
312-321-7710
Mary Lu Linnane, Head of Technical Services
In order to participate in the LCS (Library Computer System) project in Illinois, the DePaul Law Library had to convert all its records to machine-readable format. Due to the nature of legal materials and the way they are supplemented this was a somewhat unsettled problem until the actual records were available online.

DePaul University Library
2323 N. Seminary
Chicago, IL 60614
312-321-7934
Doris R. Brown, Associate Director, Technical Services
Converted 170,000 titles to full MARC form using OCLC.

DuPage Library System
PO Box 268
127 S. 1st St.
Geneva, IL 60134
312-232-8457
Richard Shurman, Library Automation Coordinator
Used Baker & Taylor data base to get MARC records plus local holdings information, generated author/title and subject COM catalogs in film and fiche formats, reformatted machine-readable data base into CLSI format. Mixed blessing.

Governors State University
University Library
Park Forest South, IL 60466
312-534-5000, ext. 2226
Mary Schellhorn, Head, Cataloging Department
The project was a full bibliographic record conversion using OCLC. Virtually all library staff members participated in the project with very little additional project-dedicated staff.

Great River Library System
515 York St.
Quincy, IL 62301
217-223-2560
Karen S. Gray, Assistant Executive Director
To prepare machine-readable data base of all materials held in the Administrative Headquarters Collection for purposes of loading into the data base of the Resource Sharing Alliance of West Central Illinois, using OCLC tapes from ILLINET.

Illinois Valley Library System
845 Brenkman Dr.
Pekin, IL 61554
309-353-4110
Linda Bills, Systems Analyst Consultant, Resource Sharing Alliance
Conversion of all films and books. The project did involve a fair proportion of original cataloging for films, since records that matched exactly were not on the OCLC data base.

Lewis & Clark Library System
PO Box 368
Edwardsville, IL 62025
618-656-3216
Donna M. Cranmer, Head, Resources/Information Services
An average of 1000 records each month have been converted on OCLC.

North Suburban Library System
200 W. Dundee
Wheeling, IL 60090
312-438-3433 – Liz Bishoff
312-459-1300 – John Ritchie
Exploring an Auto-Graphics, OCLC combination conversion.

Northeastern Illinois University Library
5500 W. St. Louis Ave.
Chicago, Il 60625
312-583-4050, ext. 471
James Wilson McGregor, Assistant University Librarian for Technical Services
Converted over 200,000 titles in-house by tagging OCLC records, which were loaded into the Illinois Library Computer System data base. Project partially funded with $81,000 grant from the Illinois Board of Higher Education. Duration: one year. Very successful project.

Northern Illinois University
Founders Memorial Library
DeKalb, IL 60115
815-753-0528

Elaine Rast, Head, Automated Records
Began non-MARC input in university computer of entire collection in 1973. Joined OCLC in 1975. Used Electronic Keyboarding, Inc. for input of remainder of items in truncated format for statewide Library Computer System. This is *not* a recommended procedure for conversion.

River Bend Library System
PO Box 125
Coal Valley, IL 61240
309-799-3155
Mary Anne Stewart, Head, Processing Department
Our original plan was to convert our complete collection on OCLC to receive archival tapes which could be used when we purchased an automated circulation system. We discontinued our project because we did not have any funds to pay the charges.

Shawnee Library System
Greenbriar Rd.
Carterville, IL 62901
618-985-3711
Barbara G. Preece, Coordinator of Automated Services
In retrospect we should have used a vendor! With regard to efficiency, a vendor is the way to achieve the goal.

Southern Illinois University
School of Medicine Library
801 N. Rutledge St.
Springfield, IL 62702
217-782-2658
Richard Dilley, Head of Technical Services
Our experienced opinion is that the retrospective conversion of catalog records of a *medical* library is not comparable to that of a public or general academic collection, in which the record is usually located within OCLC and is acceptable as found.

Southern Illinois University at Carbondale
Morris Library
Carbondale, IL 62901
618-453-2681
Darrell L. Jenkins, Director of Library Services
We are converting approximately 490,000 records for monographs and 50,000 records for serials and periodicals into machine-readable form via OCLC.

Starved Rock Library System
900 Hitt St.
Ottawa, IL 61350
815-434-7537
DiAnn S. Iverson, Technical Services Librarian

Retrospective conversion to OCLC was the third phase of a project involving weeding and inventorying a collection of 150,000 items, approximately two-thirds of which were in circulation. As funding became a problem it became necessary to be more selective as to how much of the collection could be converted.

Suburban Library System
125 Tower Dr.
Burr Ridge, IL 60521
312-325-6640
Joanne Klene, Support Services Director
Upgrading circulation data base (35 libraries' holdings) from brief record by matching with MARC record in vendor's data base. Will probably use Auto-Graphics Inc. Contract not yet signed.

University of Chicago Library
1100 E. 57th St.
Chicago, IL 60637
312-962-8743
Richard C. Pollard, Assistant Director for Technical Services
Pilot project to support merging of John Crerar Library and University of Chicago collections in science, technology and medicine. Conversion will be accomplished using online connection to the Library of Congress data base; records will be distributed through LC/MARC service.

University of Illinois at Chicago
PO Box 8198
Chicago, IL 60680
312-996-2716
Beverly P. Lynch, University Librarian
Converted records on OCLC for statewide Library Computer System.

Western Illinois University Libraries
Western Ave.
Macomb, IL 61455
309-298-2411
Roy Chang, Catalog Librarian
In 1980, Western Illinois University Libraries received a grant of $82,000 from the Illinois Board of Higher Education to convert the pre-OCLC cataloging records into machine-readable form in order to participate in the Illinois LCS network. As a result of the successful in-house retrospective conversion operation, our cataloging records are now in full MARC form.

INDIANA

Evansville-Vanderburgh County Public Library
22 SE Fifth St.
Evansville, IN 47708

DATA CONVERSION

812-425-2621
Michael J. Abaray, Head, Technical Services Department
We are one of five Indiana public libraries participating in the retrospective conversion project sponsored by INCOLSA (Indiana network for OCLC) and funded in part by an LSCA grant. Records in the OCLC data base are edited to agree with the book-in-hand.

Indianapolis-Marion County Public Library
PO Box 211
Indianapolis, IN 46206
317-269-1815
Susan Eberschoff-Coles, Supervisor of Technical Services
Federally funded LSCA grant through INCOLSA. Searching OCLC with book-in-hand.

Jefferson Township Public Library
PO Box 1548
Jeffersonville, IN 47130
812-282-7765
Bill Bolte, Director
We are considering the use of Carrollton Press REMARC. We began in July 1982 to do retrospective conversion via INCOLSA, but have felt it too time-consuming and costly to do retrospective conversion via OCLC non-prime time.

Lake County Public Library
1919 81st Ave. W.
Merrillville, IN 46410-5382
219-769-3541
Marcella Ciucki, Chief of Technical Services
Lake County Public Library was one of five public libraries in Indiana selected to participate in a retrospective conversion project funded by an LSCA grant for two years beginning in October 1980.

Vigo County Public Library
One Library Square
Terre Haute, IN 47807
812-232-1113
Alice L. Wert, Coordinator, Technical Services
VCPL is participating in a retrospective conversion project for creating machine-readable data bases for five major public libraries in Indiana via OCLC.

KANSAS

Central Kansas Library System
1409 Williams
Great Bend, KS 67530
316-792-2393
Norma Drees, Director of Technical Services

Used Science Press and Baker & Taylor (through the Kansas State Library). We used OCR at first. Then we used OCLC after going online with them. We added the holdings of all 50 of our libraries.

KENTUCKY

Eastern Kentucky University
John Grant Crabbe Library
Richmond, KY 40475
606-622-1708
Ling-yuh W. (Miko) Pattie, Catalog Section Chief
Our retrospective conversion project is closely associated with a reclassification project which was started in September 1975. We went online with OCLC in April 1976. Our recommendations to others would be: 1. Do a systematic weeding prior to initiating a retrospective conversion project; 2. Work on "as circulated" titles first; and 3. Offer better compensation for trained personnel to lessen turnover. We'll be glad to share our manuals and flowcharts for the project with anyone who is interested.

Western Kentucky University
Helm-Cravens Library
College Heights
Western Kentucky University
Bowling Green, KY 42101
502-745-2904
Earl Wassom, Director of Library Services and Assistant Dean of Academic Services
The reclassification to Library of Congress was designed in-house in 1971. This was a highly effective conversion.

LOUISIANA

Loyola University Library
6363 St. Charles Ave.
New Orleans, LA 70118
504-865-3346
Darla H. Rushing, Head of Cataloging
We have been using the OCLC system for in-house conversion and have converted approximately 20,000 titles.

McNeese State University
Frazar Memorial Library
Lake Charles, LA 70609
318-477-2520, ext. 265
Carolyn Ringle, Head, Catalog Department
Our project is primarily a reclassification project in which we are changing from the Dewey Decimal classification to the Library of Congress scheme. We are using the OCLC system. Our biggest problems have centered around the changes caused by *AACR2*.

New Orleans Public Library
219 Loyola Ave.
New Orleans, LA 70140
504-524-7382, ext. 61
Regina O. Matthews, Head, Cataloging and Processing
OCLC member since 1975. SOLINET preprocessed initial load of 72,000 records. NOPL is an ALIS II (DataPhase) library.

University of New Orleans
The Earl K. Long Library
Lake Front
New Orleans, LA 70148
504-286-6197
Donald D. Hendricks, Dean of Library Services
In 1976 began to convert 318,000 shelflist records, merging them into the OCLC data base. Currently have 91,000 entries converted. The project was, generally, not successful.

MAINE

Portland Public Library
5 Monument Square
Portland, ME 04101
207-773-4761
Bonnie Taylor, Head, Technical Services
Two office assistants in Technical Services spend about two hours each day adding our holding symbol to existing records in OCLC. PPL also has done a retrospective conversion project in building its CLSI circulation system data base.

MASSACHUSETTS

C/W Mars
(Central/Western Massachusetts Automated Resource Sharing)
c/o Anna Maria College
Mendor-Eagen Library
Paxton, MA 01612
617-757-4586, ext. 326
David Sheehan, Network Manager
Twenty-six institution, multi-type circulation. Each library does its own input.

University of Massachusetts
Joseph P. Healey Library
Harbor Campus
Boston, MA 02125
617-929-7622
Robert L. Patterson, Systems Librarian
Our OCLC retrospective conversion backlog is frozen at 222,448 titles.

MINNESOTA

Concordia College
Carl B. Ylvisaker Library
Moorhead, MN 56560
218-299-4640
Myron Flugstad, Catalog Librarian
About 103,000 of 150,000 bibliographic records have been converted via OCLC. The magnetic tapes holding these converted records have been added to the Mankato State University Project for Automated Library Services Online Catalog.

Great River Regional Library
405 St. Germain
St. Cloud, MN 56301
612-252-7282
David Cole, Technical Services Coordinator
Retrospective conversion of 100,000 titles, completed in 1982 via OCR forms for General Research Corp. Began OCLC in November 1982.

Hennepin County Library
Technical Services Division
1201 Ridgedale Dr.
Minnetonka, MN 55343
612-541-8530
Lois Tetzloff, Bibliographic Products Librarian
Typists keyed shelflist data using Magnetic Tape Selectric typewriters. The HCL systems staff, using the county's computer system, converted the keyed data into MARC II record format using automatic format recognition programs developed at the Institute of Library Research, University of California, Berkeley.

James Jerome Hill Reference Library
Fourth and Market Sts.
St. Paul, MN 55102
612-227-9531
Virgil F. Massman, Executive Director
Purchased MARC copy from Blackwell North America and Brodart. COM catalog produced by Brodart. Converted some 400,000+ records in the Cooperating Libraries in Consortium union catalog. Conversion through an online system such as OCLC or RLIN obviously is far better way of accomplishing the task.

Plum Creek Library System
921 Fourth Ave.
PO Box 184
Worthington, MN 56187
507-376-5803
Mr. Kevin Passe, COM Project Coordinator

Utilizing a microprocessor unit to facilitate data input, the holdings of the libraries affiliated with Plum Creek Library System were encoded into machine-readable form to accommodate production of a COM catalog by Brodart.

Western Plains Library System
224 S. First St.
Montevideo, MN 56265
612-269-5644
Robert A. Boese
Western Plains has been producing an off-line COM catalog since 1979 through General Research Corp.

MISSISSIPPI

First Regional Library
59 Commerce St.
Hernando, MS 38632
601-368-4439
James F. Anderson, Director
The initial contract was made with the Baker & Taylor Co., which subcontracted the General Research Corp. to maintain the data base.

Hinds Junior College Library
Raymond, MS 39154-0999
601-857-5261
Judy Myrick, Catalog Librarian
In January 1982, the Hinds Junior College Library began a three-year project to enter all library holdings into the OCLC data base via SOLINET. At the time the project began, we closed the existing card catalog and began production of a microfiche catalog, three times a year.

Jackson Metropolitan Library System
301 N. State St.
Jackson, MS 39201
601-944-1120
Russell Fulmer, Coordinator of Technical Services
The project began as an in-house conversion using OCLC. Later we chose the OCLC Conversion Unit of the Cataloging Services Department because of the quality of its work and its customizing inputting standards to meet our needs.

MISSOURI

St. Louis County Library
1640 S. Lindbergh Blvd.
St. Louis, MO 63131
314-994-3300
Betty Schramm, Assistant Director, Library Services

Our own staff typed catalog entries using OCR type. The typing was sent to a computer scanning company. This company created a tape from the OCR typing and sent this tape to Brodart, Inc. to process.

University of Missouri-Columbia
University Library
Columbia, MO 65201
314-882-3057
Robin Kespohl, Head, Catalog Maintenance
Shelflist drawers are shipped UPS to AMIGOS in Dallas. We are very pleased with the accuracy, speed and cooperation of AMIGOS.

University of Missouri-Columbia
University Library
Columbia, MO 65201
314-882-4656
Victor C. Myers, Head, Search/Cataloging
In-house conversion of post-1965, roman alphabet monographs that are returned from AMIGOS' Bibliographic Council as "problems." Converted internally using OCLC as the input medium.

University of Missouri-Columbia
University Library
Columbia, MO 65201
314-882-4678
J. Drew Racine, Head, Serials Project
In-house retrospective conversion of around 70,000 serial titles using OCLC. Libraries converting serials can expect to use high level support staff and at least a half-time professional serials cataloger and can expect the length of the project to be underestimated.

University of Missouri-Kansas City
General Library
5100 Rockhill Rd.
Kansas City, MO 64110
816-276-1528
Helen Spalding, Director, Technical Services
Conversion of monographs with imprint dates between 1970 and 1979 (the year the library started using OCLC), excluding music and nonprint materials. Very satisfied with service from AMIGOS.

University of Missouri-Rolla
Curtis Laws Wilson Library
Rolla, MO 65401
314-341-4227
James Cubit, Assistant Director for Technical Services
Two employees were able to convert approximately 120,000 volumes within 26 months. Of the 120,000 volumes converted on OCLC, less than 4% required cataloger attention.

University of Missouri-St. Louis
Jefferson Library
St. Louis, MO 63121
314-553-5064
Frank Sadowski, Head, Bibliographic Services
Conversion of all monographs, excluding audiovisual and microforms, using OCLC.

Washington University
School of Medicine Library
4580 Scott Ave.
St. Louis, MO 63110
314-454-3711, ext. 6
Jeanny T. Chan, Head, Cataloging Department
In April 1982 we contracted with OCLC for the conversion of 13,000 monographic records. The project was completed in six weeks with minimal technical specifications. The hit rate was 92%.

MONTANA

Lewis & Clark Library
120 S. Last Chance Mall
Helena, MT 59601
406-442-2371
Molly Herrin, Head, Processing Department
Auto-Graphics converted our shelflist in 1976. The data base information was loaded into our CLSI LIBS computer for our circulation system. In 1979 we changed our vendor to Brodart.

Miles Community College Library
2715 Dickinson
Miles City, MT 59301
406-232-3031
Larry Torstenbo, Director of Library Services
A local system, online Library Catalog System, using an IBM 34 can access items by author, title and subject. Very functional.

Montana State Library
1515 E. 6th St.
Helena, MT 59620
406-449-3115
Char LeVasseur, Catalog Librarian
The Montana State Library is using WLN's retrospective conversion process, WYLBUR.

NEBRASKA

Lincoln City Libraries
14th and N Sts.
Lincoln, NE 68508
402-435-2146

Cindy Cochran, Coordinator of Technical Processes
Our project involved converting 160,000 titles of our public library system into machine-readable form using the OCLC data base as the source.

University of Nebraska at Omaha
University Library
Omaha, NE 68182
402-554-3203
Ella Jane Bailey, Technical Services Librarian
Employees convert records to machine-readable form using OCLC. The three campuses of the University of Nebraska system used a shared bibliographic record within the DataPhase ALIS computerized circulation system.

NEVADA

Elko County Library
720 Court St.
Elko, NV 89801
702-738-3066 or 702-738-3077
Carol Madsen, Assistant Director, Head, Technical Services
An arbitrary cut-off date was chosen and retrospective conversion by LCCN, author, title, call number input via OCR was undertaken. Converting the retrospective and keeping up the current cataloging proved to be a strain on staff time. Brodart, Inc. was the vendor.

Nevada State Library
Capitol Complex
Carson City, NV 89701
701-885-5160
Joan Kerschner, Assistant State Librarian
Using General Research Corp., we are converting all holdings that will match LC card numbers via OCR. So far it is working beautifully.

Washoe County Library
PO Box 2151
Reno, NV 89505
702-785-4519
Martha B. Gould, Assistant Director
COM catalog was produced by using our CLSI circulation data base, and the CLSI tape program. We had General Research Corp. expand the titles into full cataloging. This project has been cost-effective in terms of increased productivity in the catalog department, and in our ability to cut labor-intensive tasks and to make better use of our existing staff members.

NEW MEXICO

University of New Mexico
Zimmerman Library
Albuquerque, NM 87131

505-277-3558
Chris Sugnet, Head, Bibliographic Control Department
Ours is an in-house project designed to do retrospective conversion of monographic records on OCLC in classification ranges that have had recent high circulation, the initial goal being to support a DataPhase circulation system that will go online in 1983.

NEW YORK

American Museum of Natural History
Library
Central Park W. at 79th St.
New York, NY 10024
212-873-1300
Diana Shih
Two-year project funded by an HEA Title II-C grant (1979-81) to convert approximately 20,000 records into machine-readable form using OCLC.

Brookhaven National Laboratory
Research Library
Upton, NY 11973
516-282-3480
Rosemary C. Cohen, Supervisor, Technical Services Branch, Research Library
We mailed Pro Libra approximately 40,000 shelflist cards that were searched in the OCLC data base. They added 98% of our holdings to the OCLC data base at a reasonable cost and with only a slight error rate.

New York State Library
Cultural Education Center
Empire State Plaza
Albany, NY 12230
518-474-5955
J. Van der Veer Judd, Principal Librarian, Network Services
There have been three projects. The methodology used in each project differed substantially and was tailored to the specific needs of the project.

State University Agricultural & Technical College at Delhi (SUNY)
Delhi, NY 13753
607-746-4107
Herbert J. Sorgen, Librarian
Conversion of over 56,000 records to OCLC data base.

United States Military Academy Library
Building 757
Technical Services Division
West Point, NY 10996
914-938-2373
Charles A. Ralston, Assistant Librarian for Technical Services

We are inputting all non-OCLC cataloging records (mainly pre-1974 imprints) with LC classification into the OCLC online data base, and, at the same time, building up our Geac, Inc. online circulation/catalog system. This latter effort is accomplished by receiving OCLC-MARC tapes from the SUNY-OCLC network and loading them into Geac. These tapes then overlay the Geac system to create full bibliographic records for the non-OCLC works, previously input in a brief record form at time of check-out.

Yonkers School Library System (INTERSHARE)
Library Service Center
162 McLean Ave.
Yonkers, NY 10705
914-968-8787
Adelaine S. Handelman and Helen P. York
Creation of union catalog of holdings of 35 school district libraries via OCLC. Union catalog issued on microfiche to facilitate interlibrary loan.

NORTH CAROLINA

Central North Carolina Regional Library
342 S. Spring St.
Burlington, NC 27215
919-227-2096
Margaret B. Blanchard, Director
GRC receives data from our library by means of OCR input and produces a microfiche listing of our holdings three times per year. Project is progressing slowly but very satisfactorily.

Cumberland County Public Library
215 Anderson St.
Fayetteville, NC 28302
919-483-8600
James D. Lee, Head, Technical Services
Conversion of the catalog to a full MARC format. Project included conversion of previous vendor's tapes of CCPL data base to interface with present vendor's (General Research Corp.) programs. Hit rate of 76%.

Forsyth County Public Library
660 W. 5th St.
Winston-Salem, NC 27101
919-727-2556
Robert Burgin, Associate Director
Begun in 1972. Data is keyed by Science Press from cataloging information provided by the Forsyth County Public Library staff. OCR was used briefly, but proved unsatisfactory.

Greensboro Public Library
201 N. Greene St.
Drawer X-4

Greensboro, NC 27402
919-373-2603
Ashby Wilson, Systems Librarian
We used IBM Selectric typewriters with OCR fonts, putting in LC card numbers and our Dewey number. We converted 91,000 bibliographic records to machine-readable form in 2½ months. Very fast, but Blackwell North America's data base is dirty.

North Carolina State Library
109 E. Jones St.
Raleigh, NC 27611
919-733-4488
Eunice P. Drum, Chief, Technical Services
Project was begun in January 1980, funded by an LSCA grant, which is renewable annually. Using the OCLC data base for the last year, we had a hit rate of 96.97%. High turnover rate of part-time staff, mainly students, has been a problem. I would prefer full-time staff with fringe benefits even if staff is smaller.

North Carolina State University
D.H. Hill Library
Box 5007
Raleigh, NC 27650
919-737-2603
Walter High, Head, Monographic Cataloging Department
Many problems uncovered during project lead to substantial recataloging and cleaning up. Since October 1976, approximately 225,000 records have been converted.

Public Library of Charlotte and Mecklenburg County
310 N. Tryon St.
Charlotte, NC 28202
704-333-4252
Emily Walker, Head, Automated Library Information System.
Conversion has taken place using OCLC Conversion Unit to edit records and then to transfer them to our ALIS (DataPhase) data base. As of January 1983, all branches fully online with ALIS.

Rockingham County Public Library
527 Boone Rd.
Eden, NC 27288
919-627-1106
Martha H. Davis, Library Director or Barbara Bolden, Technical Services Librarian
In January 1983 we are changing vendors and converting the data base to a full MARC format. Science Press was the previous vendor. General Research Corp. will be the new vendor and will convert existing data base to full MARC format. We found Science Press very cooperative to work with and are changing vendors only because Science Press has not adopted the full MARC format.

Rowan Public Library
PO Box 4039
201 W. Fisher St.
Salisbury, NC 28144
704-633-5578
Susan M. Kerr, Technical Services Librarian
Used General Research Corp. As is often the case, we rushed in the beginning, failing to take advantage of what is learned from early errors.

Wake County Public Libraries
104 Fayetteville St. Mall
Raleigh, NC 27601
919-755-6077
Antoinette Foster, Head Cataloger
Began with Brodart in late 1979 using OCR method, hitting against the MARC data base. In 1980 we received two microprocessors and used these instead of OCR. We are now converting records with Brodart access numbers on SOLINET.

OHIO

Akron-Summit County Public Library
55 S. Main St.
Akron, OH 44326
216-762-7621
Steven Hawk, Librarian-Director
Project was initiated and funded with LSCA funds by the State Library of Ohio. Grant was to OCLC which provided personnel for entire project.

Bowling Green State University
Jerome Library
Bowling Green, OH 43403
419-372-2106
Joan M. Repp, Chair, Access Services
Retrospective conversion of the shelflist using the OCLC data base. The library decided to adopt the LC classification system January 1, 1979. Reclassification of the reference collections was combined with their retrospective conversion.

Cleveland Public Library
325 Superior Ave.
Cleveland, OH 44114
216-623-2886 or 216-623-2817
Derry Juneja, Head, Catalog Department or Edward Seely, Head, Technical Services
Cleveland Public contracted with OCLC to complete conversion of remaining foreign language, adult fiction and juvenile fiction and nonfiction records. The OCLC retrospective conversion unit maintains high quality control, so we were pleased with the results of their conversion.

Cuyahoga County Public Library
4510 Memphis Ave.
Cleveland, OH 44144
216-398-1800
Virginia Lowell, Technical Services Director
OCLC Retrospective Conversion Unit added the institutional code to records, based on a match between the record and a microfilmed shelflist record. CCPL feels its conversion was done in the fastest, most economical manner possible.

Dayton and Montgomery County Public Library
215 E. Third St.
Dayton, OH 45402
513-224-1651
Timothy G. Kambitsch, Supervisor, Automated Library System
Retrospective conversion through Electronic Keyboarding Inc. EKI found that the sound recording records were much more complicated and were much longer than it had anticipated and asked the library to renegotiate the terms of the project.

Public Library of Columbus and Franklin County
28 South Hamilton Rd.
Columbus, OH 43213
614-864-8050
Richard Palmer, Director of Technical Services
OCLC received an LSCA grant to do a retrospective conversion of the adult nonfiction holdings of the major metropolitan libraries in Ohio.

The State Library of Ohio
65 South Front St.
Columbus, OH 43215
614-462-7061
Richard M. Cheski, State Librarian
Records for The State Library were input from 14 microfilm reels of the title catalog on OCLC. The State Library of Ohio discarded its card catalog on April 2, 1982 and became the first State Library in the nation with an online public catalog.

Toledo-Lucas County Public Library
325 Michigan St.
Toledo, OH 43624
419-255-7055
Betsy Isphording, Head, Processing Department
The State Library of Ohio contracted with OCLC for the conversion of bibliographic records of all adult nonfiction titles held in this and other major public libraries in Ohio.

University of Akron
School of Law Library
C. Blake McDowell Law Center
Akron, OH 44325
216-375-7447

Kyle Passmore, Assistant Law Librarian, Technical Services
We are searching the OCLC data base for records of our older materials and updating those records that we find.

University of Cincinnati Libraries
Burnam Classics Library
Cincinnati, OH 45221
513-475-5652
Patricia T. Rine, Head, Catalog Department
OCLC will begin converting Classics Library Collection by the end of January 1983, to end by December 1983. Central Catalog Department to begin converting other materials by February 1, 1983. This project will continue through at least 1984.

Upper Arlington Public Library
2800 Tremont Rd.
Columbus, OH 43221
614-486-0900
Carl A. Anderson, Head, Automation Department
Placing entire collection into data base. Using full MARC records. The transition from Regiscope to Virginia Tech Library System is in process.

Westerville Public Library
126 South State St.
Westerville, OH 43081
614-882-7277
Esther M. Turoci, Head, Technical Services
Converted approximately 80,000 titles in order to receive bar coded labels for Gaylord automated circulation system. Now using same data to convert to Virginia Polytechnic Institute's VTLS along with the Public Library of Columbus and Franklin County and the Worthington Public Library. Approximately 38,007 records were input for us by OCLC's Retrospective Conversion Unit.

Youngstown State University
William F. Maag Library
410 Wick Ave.
Youngstown, OH 44555
216-742-3675
Angela Mudrak, Librarian, Technical Services
Using OCLC online catalog.

OKLAHOMA

Metropolitan Library System
131 Dean A. McGee Ave.
Oklahoma City, OK 73102
405-631-1149
Beverly J. Sprehe, Head of Cataloging
With the successful completion of our project and the implementation of the OCLC ILL Subsystem, access to our resources has been readily available to the state and nation.

Oklahoma Department of Libraries
200 NE 18th
Oklahoma City, OK 73105
405-521-2502
Beverly L. Jones, Chief Planning Officer
Shelflist cards were shipped to AMIGOS. They entered holding symbol on appropriate OCLC record.

Oral Roberts University Library
7777 South Lewis
Tulsa, OK 74171
918-495-6883
Max Moore, Assistant Director, Library Computer Services
In 1978 the vast majority of ORU's library collection was converted into machine-readable form through the use of four OCLC CRTs. Records not found on OCLC (a small percentage of the total) were either put into OCLC as new cataloging, or were converted into machine-readable form using OCR scan sheets.

University of Oklahoma Libraries
Norman, OK 73019
405-325-4081
Janice Donnell, Head of Cataloging
Using students who were supervised by full time staff, a retrospective conversion project using OCLC resulted in the conversion of approximately 150,000 bibliographic records. The students did an excellent job. We felt this approach was very cost effective and the quality of input extremely high.

PENNSYLVANIA

Academy of Natural Sciences of Philadelphia
19th and the Parkway
Philadelphia, PA 19103
215-299-1040
Barbara Weir, Head Cataloger
Conversion of shelflist into OCLC. The project demonstrated that a research library may have special needs and practices which should be taken into account in planning the project.

Beaver County Federated Library System
2020 Main St.
Aliquippa, PA 15001
412-378-0585
Joseph C. Palmer, Coordinator
The Retrospective Conversion Project of Beaver County was LSCA funded. Auto-Graphics, Inc. was the vendor. The Retrospective Conversion Project was a two-year project which had a COM catalog as the final product.

Carnegie Library of Pittsburgh
4400 Forbes Ave.
Pittsburgh, PA 15213
412-622-3127
Joseph Falgione, Associate Director, Central Readers Services
Since January 1973 all cataloging of new material (LC) added to our collection has been entered in the OCLC data base.

Centre County Library & Historical Museum
203 N. Allegheny St.
Bellefonte, PA 16823
814-355-1516
Gary D. Wolfe, District Center Administrator
This is a retrospective conversion project in which the holdings of the Centre County Library & Historical Museum and the Schlow Memorial Library will be converted into machine-readable format using OCLC.

Clearfield County Public Library Federation
458 State St.
Curwensville, PA 16833
814-236-0589
Diane L. Pellerite, Director; Jackie Appleton, Assistant Cataloger
OCLC produces and sends Clearfield County's tapes to Pittsburgh Regional Library Center (PRLC), which strips our holdings off and puts them on tape. This tape is then sent to General Research Corp. which maintains our holdings and makes a fiche which is sent to us.

The Free Library of Philadelphia
19th and Vine Sts.
Philadelphia, PA 19103
215-686-5340
Frances Hinton, Chief, Processing Division
Approximately 500,000 cards for all formats from the official main entry catalog were sent to OCLC Retrospective Conversion Service for conversion. Detailed specifications are available. The hit rate was approximately 88%.

Lancaster County Library
125 North Duke St.
Lancaster, PA 17602
717-394-2652
Suzanne E. Hamme, Project Coordinator
We are adding approximately 100,000 titles to our archival tapes produced by OCLC. The entire process—reclassifying, recataloging, relabeling and inputting—is taking longer than we had anticipated.

Pennsylvania State University
University Libraries
University Park, PA 16802
814-865-1850
Gordon Rowlins, Director
Library Information Access System (LIAS) was designed in-house as a fully integrated library system using Honeywell hardware.

SOUTH CAROLINA

Greenville County Library
300 College St.
Greenville, SC 29601
803-242-5000
Charles A. Stevenson, Coordinator for Technical Services
Funded by CETA, the retrospective conversion project was undertaken to produce a COM catalog through Brodart, Inc., to replace the card catalog and give our branches their first catalog. Typing complete entries in the beginning would have saved us time and many complications.

Richland County Public Library
1400 Sumter St.
Columbia, SC 29210
803-799-9084
Linda Allman, Chief, Technical Services
Conversion on OCLC began August 1979 and is projected to be finished June 30, 1984. Inventory was not taken prior to conversion. The last inventory was more than 15 years ago. Many titles converted may be missing or in poor condition.

South Carolina State Library
1500 Senate St.
PO Box 11469
Columbia, SC 29211
803-758-3181
Marjorie A. Mazur, Director of Technical Services
Titles are being added by classifications we feel will be of most benefit to the libraries of our state. Conversion done on OCLC.

Spartanburg County Public Library
333 S. Pine St.
PO Box 2409
Spartanburg, SC 29304
803-596-3507
Dennis L. Bruce, Director
Converted holdings to a short title format for a CL Systems, Inc. LIBS 100 circulation system.

Winthrop College Library
Winthrop College
Rock Hill, SC 29733
803-323-2131
Carole R. McIver, Head, Technical Services Division; Alan M. Greenberg, Head, Cataloging Department
Conversion on OCLC began in September 1976 with 173,070 monograph titles and as of December 22, 1982, there were approximately 4527 of these left to convert. Concentration has been on monographs in the general collection but plans are to convert all library materials except government documents.

SOUTH DAKOTA

Historical Resource Center
500 E. Capitol
Memorial Building
Pierre, SD 57501
605-773-3615
Rosemary Evetts, Librarian
At some time in the past, about one half of the total uncataloged items in this library were classified into the LC E-F schedules. My retrospective conversion involved reclassifying all those items into the appropriate schedules and standardizing the description and subject headings.

Mount Marty College Library
1105 W. 8th St.
Yankton, SD 57078
605-668-1558
Barbara Haley, Cataloger
We were engaged in a retrospective conversion project until OCLC started charging for updating. When we were updating, we were doing so with the idea of cooperating with other libraries in our consortium for interlibrary loan.

Northern State College
Williams Library
Aberdeen, SD 57401
605-622-2645
E.J. McNeer, Director
Existing staff and CETA employee converted entire collection in 3 years.

Rapid City Public Library
610 Quincy
PO Box 3090
Rapid City, SD 57701
605-394-4171
Bruce Mehlhaff, Associate Library Director

We are entering our records on the OCLC data base using our regular library staff and no additional equipment. We are by no means experts on the subject of retrospective conversion, but will be happy to share our experiences with others.

Sioux Falls College
Norman B. Mears Library
Sioux Falls, SD 57101
605-331-6662
Evelyn Olson, Assistant Librarian
The greatest progress in retrospective conversion was accomplished in 1977 and 1978 with student assistance.

TENNESSEE

Chattanooga-Hamilton County Bicentennial Library
1001 Broad St.
Chattanooga, TN 37402
615-757-5320
Kathryn Arnold, Director of Library
To input into the OCLC data base the library's holdings in the Business, Science and Technology, and Fine Arts Collections, and special collections of Chattanooga/Hamilton County history and genealogical materials of the southeast. Project is part of statewide effort to establish an automated data base of libraries in Tennessee.

Memphis-Shelby County Public Library and Information Center
1850 Peabody Ave.
Memphis, TN 38104
901-528-2963
Jan Neal, Automated Systems Liaison
Two OCLC terminals are dedicated to the retrospective conversion project during SOLINET's low-rate hours. Approximately 258,000 records have been entered in four years.

Memphis State University Libraries
Memphis State University
Memphis, TN 38152
901-454-2201
Annelle R. Huggins, Coordinator of Technical Services
The Database Development Section of the Catalog Department is responsible for the conversion of the shelflist via OCLC.

ORNL Library System
Oak Ridge National Laboratory
PO Box X, 4500N
Oak Ridge, TN 37830
615-574-6731
Cathryn R. Nook, Head of Technical Services

Retrospective conversion of the ORNL Library System's card catalog, using OCLC, converted 70,000 monographic and 10,000 serial records. Data from SOLINET's LAMBDA will be loaded into the library's acquired Computerized Library System for online circulation and online catalog.

Public Library of Nashville and Davidson County
222 8th Ave. North and Union
Nashville, TN 37203
615-244-4700
Gene Kittrell, Head, Catalog Division
We are working to convert 170,000 titles representing 530,000 volumes, through OCLC. Incentive and enthusiasm of the participants have been sustained—they feel rewarded for competency in an area in which they are particularly qualified.

Southern Missionary College
McKee Library
PO Box 629
Collegedale, TN 37315
615-396-4297
Peg Bennett, Assistant Librarian, Head Cataloging Department
We try to confine our retrospective conversion to non-prime OCLC time which greatly slows completion of the project. However, SOLINET, as a part of its LAMBDA project, plans to offer some assistance in retrospective conversion in the near future.

Southwestern at Memphis
Burrow Library
2000 N. Parkway
Memphis, TN 38112
901-274-1800, ext. 365
Emily Flowers, Catalog Librarian
Our project is minor with only 2500-3000 titles converted each year by regular cataloging department in non-prime hours on OCLC. We hope at some point to have funding to complete the project.

University of Tennessee at Chattanooga
UTC Library
615 McCallie Ave.
Chattanooga, TN 37402
615-755-5403
Susan H. Pinckard, Head, Cataloging Department
UTC began retrospective conversion in September 1981 upon completion of its reclassification project. Seventy-five percent of cataloging staff/terminal time is given to retrospective conversion; remaining 25% given to reference, serials and audiovisuals. New monographs are allowed to backlog.

TEXAS

Austin Public Library
PO Box 2287
Austin, TX 78768-2287
512-472-5433
Sharon Justice, Head, Technical Services or Bonnie Juergens, Head, Library Data Processing
One hundred and ten thousand records have been updated in the OCLC data base. The DOBIS data base serves as an online catalog for staff and as the basis for a COM catalog for public use.

McClelland Engineers, Inc.
Corporate Library
PO Box 740010
Houston, TX 77274
713-772-3700, ext. 5305
Pat M. Johnson, Senior Librarian
Converted 5000 special library titles to the OCLC data base. Some aspects of the project were successful, some were awful. Kept extremely accurate statistics on input and financial data. This would be useful information for other special libraries, and I would be glad to share it.

University of Texas at Austin
General Libraries
PO Box P
Austin, TX 78712
512-471-5879
Sue Phillips, Assistant Director for Bibliographic Control
Converted bibliographic records for 23,000 Latin American serial titles through OCLC, with funding provided by three HEA Title II-C grants.

The University of Texas of El Paso
The Library
El Paso, TX 79968
915-747-5831
Clarence Nelson, Head, Catalog Department
The library has approximately 36,000 records to convert on OCLC. We are devoting five hours each week to retrospective conversion, and we are averaging 250 updates each month.

UTAH

University of Utah
Marriott Library
Salt Lake City, UT 84112

801-581-7741
Robert P. Holley, Assistant Director for Technical Services
The retrospective conversion of materials in the Marriott Library shelflist began in 1976 via OCLC.

VIRGINIA

Virginia Beach Public Library
Municipal Center
Room 310, Operations Building
Virginia Beach, VA 23456
804-481-6096
Rheda Epstein, Supervising Librarian
Began OCR input training by Brodart staff in August 1978. Began cataloging on OCLC via SOLINET in November 1981. All current cataloging is done on OCLC with weekly OCLC tapes being sent to Brodart to produce our bi-monthly COM catalog tapes. Very satisfied with Brodart as a vendor.

CAVALIR (Catalog of Virginia Library Resources) is the state union list. The online system was developed by The Computer Company under a state contract. The data base used for matching was derived from archival tapes from all OCLC members in Virginia plus the LC MARC data base. The system may be searched by author/title key or by LCCN, ISBN or vendor number. More than 1.2 million records in 20 libraries have been converted. An original cataloging module allows libraries to add titles not in the data base. More than 19,300 titles have been originally cataloged since May 1982. Libraries involved have ranged in size from 20,000 to 300,000 titles. They have included college, community college and public libraries. Representatives of these libraries are listed below.

Alexandria Library
717 Queen St.
Alexandria, VA 22314
703-838-4558
Marjorie Tallichet, Deputy Director

Amherst County Public Library
PO Box 370
Amherst, VA 24521
804-946-5260
Leona E. Doggett, Director

Blue Ridge Regional Library
310 E. Church St.
Martinsville, VA 24112
703-632-7125
McCluer Sherrard, Cataloger

Central Rappahannock Regional Library
1201 Caroline St.
Fredericksburg, VA 22401
703-371-3311
Bonnie M. Isaksen, Head of Cataloging

George Mason University
Fenwick Library
4400 University Dr.
Fairfax, VA 22030
703-323-2890
Agnes Mao, Cataloging Librarian

Lynchburg Public Library
914 Main St.
Lynchburg, VA 24504
804-847-1565
Judith Vogelback, Technical Services Librarian

New River Community College Library
PO Drawer 1127
Dublin, VA 24084
703-674-4121, ext. 339
Roberta S. White, Librarian

Newport News (VA) Public Library System
2400 Washington Ave.
Newport News, VA 23607
804-247-1504
Patricia Anderson, Head of Technical Services

Norfolk Public Library
301 E. City Hall Ave.
Norfolk, VA 23510
804-441-2428
Ralph A. Carlson, Head, Processing Department

Pamunkey Regional Library
PO Box 119
Hanover, VA 23069
804-798-6081, ext. 285
Ditter Sayers, Technical Services Librarian

Portsmouth Public Library
601 Court St.
Portsmouth, VA 23704
804-393-8501
Dean Burgess, Director

Roanoke City Public Library System
706 S. Jefferson St.
Roanoke, VA 24016
703-981-2476
Alfred T. Whitelock, City Librarian

Sweet Briar College
Mary Helen Cochran Library
Sweet Briar, VA 24595
804-381-5874
Patricia Wright, Associate Director

Virginia State Library
11th & Capitol Sts.
Richmond, VA 23219
804-786-2321
Barbara Thiele, Public Library Consultant

WEST VIRGINIA

Marshall University Libraries
Huntington, WV 25701
304-696-3102
Kenneth T. Slack, Director of University Libraries
We did retrospective conversion only when we were caught up on cataloging during our first year on OCLC. Retrospective conversion will only be accomplished as titles circulate.

West Virginia Library Commission
Cultural Center
Charleston, WV 25305
304-348-3978
Judith M. Prosser, Head, Technical Services
Created union catalog of all libraries in state using matching with MARC and original keying. Will probably use REMARC for conversion of older records. Also using MINI MARC for in-house retrieval of MARC.

West Virginia University Library
West Virginia University
Morgantown, WV 26506
304-293-4060
Evelyn M. Kocher, Chief Catalog Librarian
Monograph and serial conversion of the Physical Sciences Library. Serial conversion is in cooperation with PAULS (Pennsylvania Union List of Serials).

WISCONSIN

Oshkosh Public Library
106 Washington Ave.
Oshkosh, WI 54901

414-424-0473
Karen Boehning, Head, Technical Services
Temporary clerical personnel were hired from an agency to do a retrospective conversion project on OCLC.

Todd Wehr Library
8701 Watertown Plank Rd.
Box 26509
Milwaukee, WI 53226
414-257-8323
Darel Robb, Associate Director for Collection Development
We are inputting into OCLC all titles of books acquired before we went on OCLC in 1978.

University of Wisconsin-Eau Claire
William D. McIntyre Library
Park & Garfield
Eau Claire, WI 54701
715-836-3715
Cheryl Cutsforth, Head Cataloger
Conversion using OCLC was begun in May 1980 with a projected completion date of May 1985. It is essential that limited term staff hired specifically for a conversion project be as well trained and supervised as are members of the permanent staff.

University of Wisconsin-Green Bay
Library Learning Center
2420 Nicolet Dr.
Green Bay, WI 54301
414-465-2537
Dorma Bartlett, Assistant Director for Bibliographic Operations
The project was done on OCLC over four years. Early in the project our hit rate was about 85%. As more libraries undertook retrospective conversion projects the hit rate was about 95%.

University of Wisconsin-Parkside Library
Learning Center
Box 2000
Kenosha, WI 53141
414-553-2167
Barbara Baruth, Head of Technical Services
The project involves the use of several specially trained students to match shelflist records with OCLC records, then edit and update the OCLC records.

Waukesha County Technical Institute Library-ERC
800 Main St.
Pewaukee, WI 53072
414-548-5316
Mary Howard, Library Specialist
The WCTI Library began retrospective conversion via OCLC in 1982. A magnetic tape will be created to use for an online catalog.

WYOMING

University of Wyoming Library
Box 3334, University Station
Laramie, WY 82071
307-766-3279
William L. Stewart, Associate Director for Technical Services
A project to convert approximately 256,000 bibliographic records cataloged in LC into MARC format, adding local classification numbers and location symbols. To be completed by June 30, 1984 by Biblio Techniques for Carrollton Press.

Wyoming State Library
Supreme Court Building
Cheyenne, WY 82002
307-777-7281
Mary Sue Streeper, Head, Bibliographic Services
Since 1976, the Wyoming State Library has been collecting Library of Congress Card Numbers (LCCNs) from the public, community college and university libraries in the State. Those LCCNs and locations collected before September 1981 were sent to Brodart for full MARC records. For those items which Brodart cannot provide full bibliographic records, we anticipate sending them to Carrollton Press to pass against the REMARC data base.

Appendix B: Consultants on Data Conversion

Carl A. Anderson
Upper Arlington Public Library
2800 Tremont Rd.
Upper Arlington, OH 43221
614-486-9621
Consulted and lectured on retrospective conversion for INCOLSA, OHIONET and OCLC.

R.L. Avery
802 Moultrie Rd.
Albany, GA 31705
Directed Dougherty County (Albany, GA) Public Library's conversion project.

Carol A. Berger
C. Berger and Co.
0-N469 Purnell St.
Wheaton, IL 60187
312-653-1115
Consulting in information management. Editing for conversion projects.

Linda Bills
Bibliographic Manager & Systems Analyst
Resource Sharing Alliance of West Central Illinois
c/o Illinois Valley Library System
845 Brenkman
Pekin, IL 61554
309-353-4110
Directed the conversion of Illinois Valley Library System via OCLC.

Elizabeth Bishoff
Ela Area Public Library District
13 S. Buesching Rd.
Lake Zurich, IL 60047
312-438-3433
Designed the conversion project for North Suburban (IL) Library System.

Julia Blixrud
Minnesota Interlibrary Telecommunication Exchange
30 Wilson Library
309 19th Ave. S.
University of Minnesota
Minneapolis, MN 55455
612-373-4559
Networking, retrospective conversion training and serial union listing.

Marjorie Bloss
Rochester Regional Research Library Council
339 East Ave., Room 300
Rochester, NY 14604
716-232-7930
OCLC conversion and serial union listing.

David Brunell
SLC/Fedlink
Library of Congress
Washington, DC 20540
202-287-6055
Experienced with conversion projects, especially serial union listing.

Scott Bruntjen
Pittsburgh Regional Library Center
Beatty Hall
Chatham College
Pittsburgh, PA 15232
412-441-6409
OCLC Network Director, grant requests and data conversion.

Ruth C. Carter
G-49 Hillman Library
University of Pittsburgh
Pittsburgh, PA 15260
412-624-4673
Serial union listing and data conversion.

Maurice J. Freedman
Westchester Library System
8 Westchester Plaza
Elmsford, NY 10523
(914) 592-8214
Acted as consultant for Memphis-Shelby County (TN) Public Library and Information Center.

D. Kaye Gapen
University of Alabama
Amelia Gayle Gorgas Library, Box S
University, AL 35486
205-348-7561
Recommended as consultant by Trinity College Library.

Carolyn M. Gray
Brandeis University
Goldfarb Library
415 South St.
Waltham, MA 02254
617-647-2501
OCLC conversion leader at Western Illinois University.

Bonnie Juergens
Justan Enterprises
PO Box 33160
Austin, TX 78764
512-288-2072
Management consulting and automated information services for local government, private enterprise and libraries.

Dawn Lamade
Southeastern Library Network
400 Colony Square
Plaza Level
1201 Peachtree St., NE
Atlanta, GA 30361
404-892-0943
OCLC conversion.

Dan Lester
University of New Mexico
General Library
Albuquerque, NM 87131
505-277-4241
Consultant for University of New Mexico's conversion.

Barbara Markuson
Indiana Cooperative Library Services Authority
1100 West 42nd St.
Indianapolis, IN 46208
317-926-3361
All OCLC subsystems and all MARC formats.

Rob McGee
RMG Consultants, Inc.
PO Box 5488
Chicago, IL 60680
312-321-0432
Was consultant for Plum Creek (MN) Library System.

Frances McNamara
NELINET, Inc.
385 Elliott St.
Newton, MA 02164
617-969-0400
OCLC conversion.

Bruce Miller
SLC/Fedlink
Library of Congress
Washington, DC 20540
202-287-6055
Contracts for merging computer tapes.

Gary M. Pitkin
Associate University Librarian for Technical Services
Appalachian State University
Boone, NC 28608
704-262-2186
Has designed conversion projects for Wheaton College (IL) and for Southern Illinois University at Edwardsville.

Ellen Rappaport
State University of New York
SUNY/OCLC Network
State University Plaza (at Broadway for UPS)
Albany, NY 12246
518-474-1685
OCLC conversion.

Elaine Rast
Founders Memorial Library
Northern Illinois University
DeKalb, IL 60115
815-753-0528
Experience with local input, OCLC and EKI. Serials union listing.

Dennis Reynolds
Bibliographical Center for Research
1777 S. Bellaire, Suite G-150
Denver, CO 80222
303-691-0550
Trains staff for conversion projects. Experienced with merging records from different institutions.

Gary M. Ross
Head Librarian, Automated Cataloging
The General Libraries
The University of Texas at Austin
Austin, TX 78712
512-471-3336
OCLC experience at Ohio State as well as at UTA.

Susan Saunders
AMIGOS Bibliographic Center
11300 N. Central Expressway, Suite 321
Dallas, TX 75243
214-750-6130
OCLC conversion and serial union listing.

Arlene Schwartz
ILLINET Bibliographic Data Base Service
Illinois State Library
Centennial Building
Springfield, IL 62756
217-785-1532
Experienced with networking, serial union listing, training technical services staff.

Kenneth Simon
University of South Carolina
Thomas Cooper Library
Columbia, SC 29208
803-777-5228
Consultant for Georgia Southern College Library.

Andrew Wang
OCLC Retrospective Conversion Service
6565 Frantz Rd.
Dublin, OH 43017
800-848-5800 or 800-282-7306 (Ohio)
OCLC conversion of all MARC formats.

Appendix C: Vendors of Data Conversion Services

ALIS. See *DataPhase*

AMIGOS Bibliographic Resource Center
11300 N. Central Expressway, Suite 321
Dallas, TX 75243
214-750-6130
Susan Saunders, Director
AMIGOS offers retrospective conversion of library catalogs, including bibliographic information and local holdings data, into machine-readable form to its member libraries.

Auto-Graphics, Inc.
751 Monterey Pass Rd.
Monterey Park, CA 91754
213-269-9451
Jean M. Rado, Marketing Communications
AGILE II is an online bibliographic conversion and file maintenance system. AGILE II users have access to the MARC data base, to their own master file and to the data bases of other system users. In addition to MARC, the AGILE II data base contains approximately three million titles in MARC II format.

The bibliographic records are indexed by LC card number, author, title and keyword in the title. Matches are added to the user's own AGILE II data base and at that time may be modified bibliographically and/or have holdings and copy level information added. The user's data base may be augmented with other machine-readable records; for example, circulation system data or book jobber data. The resulting library data base can be used to produce COM catalogs, load circulation systems, etc.

Automated Library Information System (ALIS). See *DataPhase*

Avatar Systems, Inc.
11325 Seven Locks Rd., Suite 205
Potomac, MD 20854
301-983-8900
R.S. Dick
The Integrated Library System (ILS) has a comprehensive online catalog, circulation tracking, MARC cataloging and authority control, serials control and management reports, all integrated into one system.

Bibliographic Retrieval Services, Inc. (BRS)
1200 Rt. 7
Latham, NY 12110
BRS Customer Service: 518-783-1611
Online bibliographic data bases using BRS/Search retrieval software.

Blackwell North America, Inc. (BNA)
6024 SW Jean Rd., Building G
Lake Oswego, OR 97034
Dan Miller, Account Manager, Technical Services
BNA performs retrospective conversions using a master file of more than three million records. For turnkey conversions, BNA performs all searching and keying. If the library performs the conversion, BNA accepts search keys via OCR or magnetic tape. When the conversion is complete, it offers name and subject authority control services based on Library of Congress authority files. COM and paper catalog production are also offered.

BNA. See *Blackwell North America*

Brodart, Inc.
Library Automation Division
PO Box 3024
1609 Memorial Ave.
Williamsport, PA 17705
800-233-8467 or 717-326-2461
Joan M. Morgan, Eastern Regional Sales Manager
Brodart offers several different methods for the conversion of data to machine-readable form. The least expensive is OCR. Brodart supplies a special type font and forms. From the library's shelflist, the staff keys a short entry. Resource data bases are searched to retrieve full entries and edit listings are produced. This method is appropriate for libraries with clerical support and limited budgets. To improve the speed and accuracy of conversion, Brodart offers a line of microcomputer software systems called Microcheck. The conversion data can be transmitted to Brodart by mail, phone or online, using a personal computer compatible with the Microcheck Software.

BRS. See *Bibliographic Retrieval Services, Inc.*

C. Berger and Co.
0-N469 Purnell St.
Wheaton, IL 60187
312-653-1115
Carol Berger
Provides library or information system support on an "as needed" basis. Special assignments: conducting inventories; weeding files, shelves; editing for conversion projects, publications; reclassifying books and many more library services.

California Library Authority for Systems and Services (CLASS)
1415 Koll Circle
San Jose, CA 95112
408-289-1756
Libby Trudell
The Washington Library Network (WLN) and the California Library Authority for Systems and Services (CLASS) have announced the signing of an agreement making CLASS the exclusive broker for WLN's retrospective conversion services in California, Nevada, Arizona and Utah. The service compliments the RLIN shared cataloging services offered by CLASS, and provides a new option for retrospective conversion for all libraries in the four state area.

Carrollton Press, Inc. REMARC Division
1031 Executive Parkway Dr., Suite 110
St. Louis, MO 63141
314-851-9463 or 800-368-3008
K. Lee Haniford, Vice-President, Midwestern Region
Carrollton Press is working on the largest library retrospective conversion project ever conceived—for the Library of Congress. These 5 million REMARC records, plus an estimated 2 million MARC records (which LC should have produced by the completion of the conversion project in late 1983) will constitute a combined data base of LC cataloging records for 7 million unique titles. In the meantime, we 1. match libraries' holdings against today's whole MARC data base, 2. match them quarterly against the REMARC data base, 3. add local data, and 4. deliver MARC format records on magnetic tape.

Cincinnati Electronics Corp.
2630 Glendale-Milford Rd.
Cincinnati, OH 45241
513-563-6000
B. Lewis
Online library control systems.

CLASS. See *California Library Authority for Systems and Services*

CLSI. See *CL Systems, Inc.*

Collection Access Systems. See *Brodart, Inc.*

The Computer Co.
PO Box 6987
1905 Westmoreland St.
Richmond, VA 23230
Beth Diggles, Marketing Representative
The Computer Company offers libraries automated cataloging services for retrospective

and ongoing cataloging, microform catalogs and related equipment and supplies. The company produces all the services it sells with company personnel, programs and equipment. The company develops products to meet library industry standards. Once a library's cataloging is converted to MARC II format, the Computer Co. can produce: magnetic tapes of bibliographic records for use on circulation systems; patron and shelflist microfiche or microfilm catalogs for individual libraries; special collection catalogs; and union catalogs for library consortia or networks.

CL Systems, Inc.
81 Norwood Ave.
Newtonville, MA 02160
617-965-6310
G.M. Razzaboni
CLSI has been building automated library systems since 1971. It provides integrated software for small, medium and large libraries, which automates circulation, acquisitions, the public catalog, film booking and reserve room functions. It can interface with a library's cataloging system to develop a complete CLSI system.

CTI Library Systems, Inc.
1455 So. State
Orem, UT 84057
801-224-1390
Vendor for Idaho Falls Public Library.

DataPhase Systems, Inc.
3770 Broadway
Kansas City, MO 64111
816-931-7927
East Coast call: 703-237-8444
The Automated Library Information System (ALIS) integrates all library functions, including circulation, technical services, acquisitions, materials and film booking, authority control, inventory, reserve rooms, and COM.

Electronic Keyboarding, Inc. (EKI)
140 Weldon Parkway
St. Louis, MO 63043
314-567-1780 or 800-325-4984
Marge Comeau, Vice-President, Customer Service
The firm is engaged primarily in keyboarding/proofreading (verification) activities that result in usable data files. More specifically, it is engaged in extensive bibliographic record conversion projects ranging from handling of circulation type (brief) records to creating full MARC bibliographic records. Over the past 10 years the firm has handled projects in the library sciences field, directory publishing market and the legal text development arena. Major clients include: The Library of Congress, New York Public Library, the University of Illinois (including numerous state supported academic institutions), Ohio Bell Telephone and numerous independent directory publishers.

GEAC Computers International, Inc.
350 Steelcase Rd. W
Markham, Ontario, Canada L3R133
416-475-0525
B. Morton
Online library automation services.

General Research Corp. (GRC)
Computer Services Division
5383 Hollister Ave.
PO Box 6770
Santa Barbara, CA 93111
805-964-7724
Vera F. Fessler, Marketing
GRC has been supplying computerized library services since 1967. It converts vendor computer tapes to create your catalog. OCR input of new entries and updates are also available. COM produced as a result of your data base input.

Innovative Interface 300
2131 University Ave., #334
Berkeley, CA 94704
415-540-0880
S. Silverstein
Did an OCLC/CLSI interface for Lincoln Trails Library System (IL).

The Integrated Library System (ILS). See *Avatar Systems, Inc.*

Library Computer System (LCS)
University of Illinois
Administrative Information Systems and Services
370 R.R.B
PO Box 4348
Chicago, IL 60680
312-996-8870
Alice Haddix, LCS Administrator
LCS is presently an online circulation system which is being expanded to an online catalog.

Library Systems & Services, Inc.
General Motors Building
1395 Piccard Dr., Suite 100
Rockville, MD 20850
800-638-8725 or 301-258-0200
Sally Shipp, Projects Director
LSSI will convert non-automated cataloging records to machine-readable form or convert bibliographic records from one machine-readable format to another. LSSI staff members use several methods to meet the differing needs and requirements of individual libraries.

Retrospective conversion services available from LSSI range from the original input of entire bibliographic records in complete MARC format to the addition of call numbers and holding codes to MARC records extracted from in-house data bases.

Maceto, Inc.
5000 Centinela Ave., Suite 332
Los Angeles, CA 90066
213-398-9172
Thomas P. Dengler
Library contractors specializing in data conversion and retrospective conversion.

MARCIVE, Inc.
PO Box 12408
San Antonio, TX 78212
512-828-9496 (call collect)
MARCIVE offers a method for the conversion of library holdings into a machine-readable data base in full MARC format suitable for COM catalog production or for loading into automated circulation or other online systems. MARCIVE can combine these data with data from the other bibliographic utilities (OCLC, RLIN, etc.) or from other vendors into a unified data base for almost any purpose.

MINI MARC. See *Library Systems & Services, Inc.*

Minnesota State University System/Project for Automated Library Systems. See *MSUS/PALS*

MSUS/PALS
Mankato State University
Memorial Library, Box 19
Mankato, MN 56001
507-389-6201
Dale Carrison
Online public catalog.

NOTIS
Northwestern University Library
Evanston, IL 60201
312-492-7004
Kenton Andersen, NOTIS Systems
A fully integrated library system including cataloging, online public catalog, acquisitions and serials check in. Operational since 1970. Already installed in the National Library of Venezuela, University of Florida and others.

OCLC Retrospective Conversion Service
6565 Frantz Rd.
Dublin, OH 43017-0702
800-848-5800 or 800-282-7306 (Ohio)
Andrew Wang, Manager
The OCLC Retrospective Conversion Service helps libraries convert their manual catalogs into machine-readable form. The service is designed to complete your retrospective conversion project quickly and to minimize the labor required of your library staff. OCLC has successfully converted files for libraries of various types and sizes. A partial list of OCLC Retrospective Conversion customers includes: Boston University Libraries, Cleveland Public Library, Smithsonian Institution, State Library of Ohio.

Online Computer Library Center. See *OCLC Retrospective Conversion Service*

Pittsburgh Regional Library Center (PRLC)
Beatty Hall
Chatham College
Pittsburgh, PA 15232-2898
412-441-6409
Scott Bruntjen, Executive Director
PRLC contracts with libraries for data conversion and retrospective conversion.

Pro Libra Associates, Inc.
106 Valley St.
South Orange, NJ 07079
201-762-0070
Margaret Bennett, President
Did conversion for the Research Library at Brookhaven National Laboratory.

Steven L. Rasdall
17335 Raymer St.
Northridge, CA 97325
213-349-2254
Vendor for Miles Community College Library, Miles City, MT.

REMARC. See *Carrollton Press, Inc.*

The Research Libraries Group, Inc. (RLG)
Jordan Quadrangle
Stanford, CA 94305
415-328-0920
Tina Kass, Director, Library Systems and Operations

In order to build sophisticated tools to help libraries maintain bibliographic control over their materials, RLG provides member libraries with an opportunity to convert manually-produced cataloging records into machine-readable form. The value of retrospective conversion to individual libraries includes providing the library with a larger data base to be used as a basis for future online catalogs; providing a library with records which are more easily maintained; providing a library with a larger file of records to be used for reference activities. As of early 1983, RLG members are in the process of completing a number of retrospective conversion projects, ranging from complete conversion of collections to conversion of specific categories of materials. In addition, three RLG libraries have added retrospective cataloging records for serials as part of projects supported by HEA Title IIC.

Ringgold Management Systems, Inc.
Box 368
Beaverton, OR 97075
503-645-3502
John F. Knapp
Microcomputer and minicomputer based library systems.

Saztec
PO Box 5527
Eugene, OR 97405
503-343-8640
Rod Slade, Manager, Library Services
Saztec's Search Key Service offers access to millions of machine-readable catalog records through a variety of resource data bases and search keys. Search Key Service enables a library to search thousands of local catalog records in a batch against a resource data base and to obtain MARC format cataloging for a large percentage of its collection.

SOLINET. See *Southeastern Library Network, Inc.*

Southeastern Library Network, Inc.
Plaza Level, 400 Colony Square
1201 Peachtree St., NE
Atlanta, GA 30361
404-892-0943
Richard James, Manager of System Operations
SOLINET will begin to offer a retrospective conversion service which will assist libraries in converting their manual card catalogs to machine-readable form. The service may utilize both SOLINET's LAMBDA data base and that of OCLC to produce MARC-compatible records in *AACR2* format. Those records not found on the SOLINET regional data base constructed for this purpose may be searched in the OCLC data base. The institutional files, which may include local call number, holdings information and other local information, can be the basis of local system data bases or the production of COM catalogs.

UTLAS
University of Toronto Library Automation Systems
80 Bloor St. W.
2nd Floor
Toronto, Ontario, Canada M5S 2V1
416-923-0890
Brian Morrell, Manager, Special Libraries Division
To assist libraries in upgrading their holdings to MARC format, UTLAS offers CATSSERVICES. The CATSSERVICES unit, located at UTLAS, consists of specially trained operators working under the supervision of an experienced cataloger. Upon request, CATSSERVICES will carry out catalog conversion or data base creation projects for large or small collections. Working from shelflist cards, the CATSSERVICES staff search the UTLAS data base of over 15 million records, make copies of records that match the shelflist cards, and add local call number and holdings information. If no match is found, CATSSERVICES will create an original MARC record based on the shelflist card information. Both derived and original records become part of a data base from which catalog products such as cards, bookform catalogs, microfiche or microfilm catalogs, or a MARC-formatted tape can be generated. Cost estimates, based on a sample of shelflist cards, are available upon request.

Virginia Polytechnic Institute and State University (VTLS)
Burruss Hall
Blacksburg, VA 24061
703-961-6122
Vinod Chachra, Director of Center for Library Automation
Fully automated cost-effective library services. Thirty installations operational.

Washington Library Network Computer Service (WLN)
Washington State Library
AJ-11
Olympia, WA 98504
206-459-6539
Bruce Berwick, Library Services
The Batch Retrospective Conversion Subsystem provides WLN participants a low cost method for adding to the online Summary Holdings File call numbers and location information for items represented by cataloging records on the WLN data base. This process is not used for current acquisitions. Holdings information for newly acquired materials is input directly online to the Summary Holdings File.

Bibliography

Aagard, James S. "An Interactive Computer-Based Circulation System: Design and Development." *Journal of Library Automation* 5 (1): 3-11 (March 1972).

American National Standards Institute. *American National Standard for Serial Holdings at the Summary Level, ANSI Z39.42—1980.* New York: American National Standards Institute, 1980.

Anable, Richard. "The Ad Hoc Discussion Group on Serials Data Bases: Its History, Current Position and Future." *Journal of Library Automation* 6 (4): 207-214 (December 1973).

———. "CONSER: Bibliographic Considerations. *Library Resources and Technical Services* 19 (4): 341-348 (Fall 1975).

Anglo-American Cataloguing Rules, 2nd ed. Chicago: American Library Association, 1978.

Barkalow, Pat. "Conversion of Files for Circulation Control." *Journal of Library Automation* 12 (3): 209-213 (September 1979).

Beckman, Margaret M. "Online Catalogs and Library Users." *Library Journal* 107 (19): 2043-2047 (November 1, 1982).

"Bibliographic Detectives." *OCLC Newsletter* 142: 9 (July 1982).

Bruntjen, Scott. "The Political, Economic, and Technological Roots of Some Legal Issues in Library Networking." *Journal of Library Administration* 3 (2): 15-27 (Summer 1982).

Buckeye, Nancy Melin. "The OCLC Serials Subsystem: Implementation Implications at Central Michigan University." *Serials Librarian* 3 (1): 31-42 (Fall 1978).

Butler, Brett; Brian Averey; and William Scholtz. "The Conversion of Manual Catalogs to Collections Data Bases." *Library Technology Reports* 14 (2): 109-206 (March/April 1978).

Carter, Ruth C. "Cataloging Decisions on Pre-AACR2 Serial Records from a Union List Viewpoint." In *Union Lists: Issues and Answers*. Ann Arbor, MI: Perian Press, 1982.

———. "Playing by the Rules—AACR2 and Serials." In *Serials Management in an Automated Age*. Westport, CT: Meckler Publishing, 1982.

———. "Shelflist." *Encyclopedia of Library and Information Science* 27: 332-336 (1979).

———. "Standards: One That's Missing." *LITA Newsletter* 8: 8 (Spring 1982).

"A Conversation with Norman Horrocks." *Technicalities* 2 (6): 10-12 (June 1982).

Corry, Emmett. *Grants for Libraries: A Guide to Public and Private Funding Programs and Proposal Writing Techniques*. Littleton, CO: Libraries Unlimited, Inc., 1982.

Crismond, Linda F. "Quality Issues in Retrospective Conversion Projects." *Library Resources and Technical Services* 25 (1): 48-55 (January/March 1981).

DeGennaro, Richard. "Libraries and Networks in Transition: Problems and Prospects for the 1980's." *Library Journal* 106: 1045-1049 (May 15, 1981).

DeKlerk, Ann. "Barcoding a Collection—Why, When, and How." *Library Resources and Technical Services* 25 (1): 81-87 (January/March 1981).

"Draft Proposed American National Standard for Serial Holdings Statements at the Detailed Level." Washington, DC: American National Standards Committee Z39, 1982 (unpublished).

Ellis, Richard. "Electronic Ordering at UTLAS: A Chronicle of Library/Book Vendor /Bibliographic Utility Cooperation." *Information Technology and Libraries* 1 (4): 343-345 (December 1982).

Ferguson, Douglas; Neal K. Kaske; Gary S. Lawrence; Joseph R. Mathews; and Robert Zich. "The CLR Public Online Catalog Study: An Overview." *Information Technology and Libraries* 1 (2): 84-97 (June 1982).

Furlong, Elizabeth J. "A Case Study in Automated Acquisitions: Northwestern University Library." *Journal of Library Automation* 13 (4): 222-240 (December 1980).

Gorman, Michael. "The Current State of Standardization in the Cataloging of Serials." *Library Resources and Technical Services* 19 (4): 301-313 (Fall 1975).

———. "Fate, Time, Occasion, Chance, and Change; or How the Machine May Yet Save LCSH." *American Libraries* 11 (9): 557-558 (October 1980).

Govan, James. "The Union Catalogue: The Objectives and Economics in Perspective." In *The Future of the Union Catalogue.* New York: Hawthorn Press, 1982.

Grosso, Katherine Thompson. "Converting a Catalog from Sears Subject Heading to the Library of Congress Subject Heading." *Illinois Libraries* 62 (7): 631-633 (September 1980).

Harrison, Tom W. and A. Patricia Miller. "On-line Interactive Serials Management at Marathon Oil Company." *Journal of Library Automation* 12 (3): 283-289 (September 1979).

Holley, Robert P. and Dale Flecker. "Processing OCLC MARC Subscription Tapes at Yale." *Journal of Library Automation* 12 (1): 88-91 (March 1979).

Horner, William C. "Processing OCLC MARC Subscription Tapes at North Carolina State University." *Journal of Library Automation* 12 (1): 91-94 (March 1979).

John, Nancy. "Preparing for Online Access: Retrospective Conversion." *Illinois Libraries* 62 (7): 618-622 (September 1980).

Johnson, Carolyn A. "Retrospective Conversion of Three Library Collections." *Information Technology and Libraries* 1 (2): 133-139 (June 1982).

Kamens, Harry H. "OCLC's Serials Control Subsystem: A Case Study." *Serials Librarian* 3 (1): 43 (Fall 1978).

Kesner, Richard M. "The Computer and the Library Environment: The Case for Microcomputers." *Journal of Library Administration* 3 (2): 33-50 (Summer 1982).

Klene, Joanne. "Conversion—A Shared Experience," *Illinois Libraries* 62 (7): 614-616 (September 1980).

Krieger, Michael T. "Retrospective Conversion at a Two-Year College." *Information Technology and Libraries* 1 (1): 41-44 (March 1982).

Lighthill, David P. "Why OCLC Is Implementing a Copyright Protection Program for the Database." *OCLC Newsletter* 144: 3 (December 1982).

McGregor, James Wilson. "LCS: Costs of Implementation and Use." *Illinois Libraries* 64 (1): 50-52 (January 1982).

McKinley, Margaret. "A Programatic Approach to Serials Data Conversion." *Serials Review* 7 (1): 85-91 (January/March 1981).

McPherson, Dorothy S.; Karen E. Coyle; and Teresa L. Montgomery. "Building a Merged Database: The University of California Experience." *Information Technology and Libraries* 1 (4): 371-380 (December 1982).

Malinconico, S. Michael. "AACR2—Costs of Implementation Deferred." *The Bookmark* 39 (4): 207-210 (Summer 1981).

―――. "The Library Catalog in a Computerized Environment." *Wilson Library Bulletin* 51 (1): 53-64 (September 1976).

――― and Paul Fasana. *The Future of the Catalog: The Library's Choices*. White Plains, NY: Knowledge Industry Publications, Inc., 1979.

Marcum, Deanna and Richard Boss. "Information Technology." *Wilson Library Bulletin* 56 (10): 765 (June 1982).

Marshall, Joan K. "The Impact of AACR2 on a Medium-Size College Library." *The Bookmark* 39 (4): 223-227 (Summer 1981).

Metz, Paul. "Integrating Automation at Virginia Tech." *Wilson Library Bulletin* 56 (4): 262 (December 1981).

Meyer, Richard W. and John L. Knapp. "COM Catalog Based on OCLC Records." *Journal of Library Automation* 8 (4): 312-321 (December 1975).

Miller, Dick R. and Karen Brewer. "Usefulness of OCLC Archive Tapes as a Basis for Local Online Systems." *Cataloging and Classification Quarterly* 2 (3/4): 77-85 (1982).

Miller, Ellen G. "Faculty Participation in Library Automation Planning." *College and Research Libraries News* 43(6): 197-199 (June 1982).

Mowery, Robert L. "The 'Trend to LC' in College and University Libraries." *Library Resources and Technical Services* 19 (4): 389-397 (Fall 1975).

"Now, Add CONSER to Your Conversation." *American Libraries* 8 (1): 21-22 (January 1977).

"OCLC to Copyright Database." *OCLC Newsletter* 144: 1, 3 (December 1982).

OCLC Newsletter 4 (January 16, 1981).

"On-line Serials Check-In Service Designed by Faxon." *Journal of Library Automation* 13 (3): 207 (September 1980).

Paul, Hiubert. "Automation of Serials Check-In: Like Growing Bananas in Greenland? Part 1." *Serials Librarian* 6 (2): 3-16 (Winter 1981).

―――. "Automation of Serials Check-In: Like Growing Bananas in Greenland? Part 2." *Serials Librarian* 6 (4): 39-62 (Summer 1982).

Pennsylvania State University. "Library Automation at the Pennsylvania State University: The LIAS System." Middletown, PA: Pennsylvania State University, October 1981.

Pierce, Anton R. *Draft Outline for the Need to Establish a MARC Format for Library Locations, Collections, and Inventory.* Blacksburg, VA: Virginia Polytechnic Institute and State University, 1981.

Potter, William Gray. "Plans for an On-line Catalog at the University of Illinois." *Resource Sharing and Library Networks* 1 (1): 53-63 (Fall 1981).

Preston, Gregory. "A Foot in Both Camps: Using RLIN and OCLC." *Library Journal* 107 (18): 1948-1949 (October 15, 1982).

Radke, Barbara and Teresa Montgomery. "Calls ISSN Project." *Serials Review* 8 (2): 65-67 (Summer 1982).

Rast, Elaine. "Conversion Strategies for a Machine-Readable Data Base at Northern Illinois University Libraries." *Illinois Libraries* 62 (7): 616-618 (September 1980).

"RLG/Local System Link Announced." Research Libraries Group, Inc., January 1982 (press release).

"Retrospective Conversion: Where Old Information Takes on New Forms." *OCLC Newsletter* 142: 8, 10-11 (July 1982).

Rice, James. "OCR for Libraries: Only a Few Years Away." *Library Journal* 106: 1603-1605 (September 1, 1981).

Rosenthal, Joseph A. "Planning for the Catalogs: A Managerial Perspective." *Journal of Library Automation* 11 (3): 192-205 (September 1978).

Runkle, Martin. "Authority in On-line Catalogs." *Illinois Libraries* 62 (7): 603-606 (September 1980).

Salmon, Stephen R. "Planning for Library Automation: The Origins of MELVYL." *Information Technology and Libraries* 1 (4): 350-358 (December 1982).

Sawyer, Jeanne. "An Archive Tape Processing System for the Triangle Research Libraries Network." *Library Resources and Technical Services* 26 (4): 362-369 (October/December 1982).

Schabel, Donald. "Experience with a Computer Produced Catalog." *Illinois Libraries* 62 (7): 609-613 (September 1980).

Schmierer, Helen F. "The Relationship of Authority Control to the Library Catalog." *Illinois Libraries* 62 (7): 599-602 (September 1980).

"Standards Gain Stature as Automated Systems Multiply." *American Libraries* 13 (8): 522 (September 1982).

"Vendor Profile: Interview with William Buchanan, Carrollton Press and REMARC Database." *Technicalities* 2 (12): 3-6, 13 (December 1982).

Veneziano, Velma. "An Interactive Computer-Based Circulation System for Northwestern University: The Library Puts It to Work." *Journal of Library Automation* 5 (2): 101-117 (June 1972).

Wassom, Earl E. and Richard A. Jones. "Bibliographic Access to Full Descriptive Cataloging with COM." *Journal of Library Automation* 11 (1): 47-53 (March 1978).

Wetherbee, Lou. "Planning a Retrospective Conversion Project." Amigos Bibliographic Council addition to [ARL] Spec Kit Number 65 (June 1980).

Willmering, William J. "Online Centralized Serials Control." *Serials Librarian* 1 (3): 243-249 (Spring 1977).

Wittorf, Robert. "ANSI Z 39.42 and OCLC." *Serials Review* 6 (2): 87-92 (April/June 1980).

Ziegman, Bruce and Brian Averey. "WLN Online Order Transmission." *Information Technology and Libraries* 1 (4): 346-348 (December 1982).

Index

AACR2. See Anglo-American Cataloguing Rules
American Library Association (ALA), 19, 31
American National Standards Institute (ANSI), 6, 19, 66
  ANSI Standard Z39, 7, 13
American National Standards Institute Standard for Serial Holdings Statements at the Detailed Level, 63
American National Standards Institute Standard for Serial Holdings Statements at the Summary Level, 63, 67, 73
Anglo-American Cataloguing Rules (AACR2), 27-28, 46, 56, 57, 61, 62, 63, 73, 95
ANSI. *See* American National Standards Institute
Authority files, 8, 9-10, 29-31

Carrollton Press, Inc., 51
Carnegie-Mellon University Libraries, 71-72
Chicago Public Library, 54
Circulation and inventory control, 10-12
Computer Output Microform (COM), 12, 18, 25, 31, 53, 55, 64, 67
COM. *See* Computer Output Microform
CONSER. *See* Serial records

Data Composition, Inc., 71
Data conversion
  basic principles of, 3-4
  budgeting for, 89-90
  contracts, 93-95
  costs, 38-39, 81-87
  funding for, 37-41
  history of, 3
  integrated systems, 4-6, 17-19, 101
  purpose of, 3
  resources, 32-41
  trends, 99-100
    See also Implementation of data conversion, Methods of data conversion, Planning for data conversion, Project analysis
De Gennaro, Richard, 27, 101
Dewey Decimal System, 3, 28, 68

Hennepin County (MN) Library, 70
Higher Education Act (HEA) Title II-C, 40, 67

Illinois Board of Higher Education, 38
Implementation of data conversion
  initial concerns, 56-57
  problems, 91-93
  scheduling staff, 90-91
Indiana University, 67
Individual items controls
  bar code and inventory, 48, 51, 52-53, 71
  labeling, 13-14, 71-72
  OCR (optical character recognition), 51, 71, 73
  standards and formats, 51
    See also Machine-readable record
International Standard Book Number (ISBN), 22
International Standard Serial Number (ISSN), 22

Library of Congress, 8, 28, 47
  Classification System, 3, 68
Library of Congress Card Number (LCCN), 22
Library of Congress Subject Headings, 28, 68
Library Services and Construction Act (LSCA), 39-40
Library Information Access System (LIAS), 56

Machine-readable record
  maintenance of, 96-97
  methods of creating, 54-56
  ownership of, 100
  use charges for, 38, 90
  See also Individual items controls
MARC (MAchine Readable Cataloging), 6-8, 22, 24, 31-32, 46, 47, 55, 68, 96
Methods of data conversion
  adding to work flow, 26, 78-79
  adding special staff, 26, 79-80
  basic, 77
  outside vendors, 26-27, 80-81
Miami University-Hamilton (OH), 46

National Center for Education Statistics, 19
National Library of Medicine (NLM), 71
National Union Catalog, 32
New Serial Titles, 66
NOTIS (Northwestern On-Line Total Integrated System), 55

OCLC. *See* Online Computer Library Center
Online Computer Library Center (OCLC), 10-11, 24, 26, 28, 32, 39, 46, 50, 51, 53, 56, 63, 66, 73, 91-92, 93, 97, 100
  Retrospective Conversion Unit, 27
  union list, 67

Pennsylvania State University Library, 27, 55-56
Pennsylvania Union List of Serials, 67
Planning for data conversion
  allowing for delays, 93
  data element selection, 22, 47, 95-96
  establishing procedures, 47-48
  specifications, 12-13, 16, 45-47
Project analysis
  defining scope, 23-25

  establishing objectives, 21-23
  establishing standards and formats, 27-32, 95-96
  staff/vendor needs, 25-27, 33-35, 49-50

REMARC, 51
Research Libraries Information Network (RLIN), 24, 26, 28, 32-40, 46, 50, 51, 56, 93
Retroarc, 97
Rice University, 39, 71
RLIN. *See* Research Libraries Information Network

Sears List of Subject Headings, 68
Serial records
  CONSER, 62-63, 65, 72
  conversion of holdings data, 65-66
  conversion issues, 61-62, 72-73
  methods of cataloging, 63
  purpose for converting, 64-65
  standards, 66-67
Special considerations
  pre-*AACR2* records, 61, 68-71
  reclassification, 61, 68, 73
  See also Individual items controls, Serial records
State Library of Pennsylvania, 92-93

Union List of Serials, 66
University of Illinois at Urbana-Champaign Library, 23
University of South Carolina, 46
University of Texas at Dallas, 54
University of Toronto Automated Library Systems (UTLAS), 28, 32
UTLAS. *See* University of Toronto Automated Systems

Virginia Polytechnic Institute and State University, 30-31

Washington Library Network (WLN), 28, 32, 56, 93, 94
Western Kentucky University, 54
WLN. *See* Washington Library Network

ABOUT THE AUTHORS

Ruth C. Carter is head of the cataloging department at the University of Pittsburgh Libraries. Previously, she was head of the serials unit of the Libraries. Ms. Carter has published articles on cataloging and library automation in several professional journals, and has been active as a consultant and speaker on data conversion. She is chairperson of the Pittsburgh Regional Library Center Ad Hoc Committee on Union List of Periodicals, and is a member of OCLC's Serials Control Advisory Committee and Union List Task Force.

Dr. Scott Bruntjen is executive director of the Pittsburgh Regional Library Center. He was previously associate professor and head of public services at the Shippensburg State College Library. Dr. Bruntjen is editor of the *PRLC Newsletter* and coauthor of *A Checklist of American Imprints.* He has been an active writer, speaker and consultant on data conversion and other aspects of library automation.

Elaine Rast is head of the automated records department at the Northern Illinois University Founders Memorial Library. Previously, she was head of the regional campuses technical services department at Ohio State University Libraries. Ms. Rast is a member of the OCLC Users Council Executive Committee. She has published articles in a number of professional journals.